# A REVIEW OF FORMAL POETRY

## VOLUME 8, ISSUE 2
## 2013

EDITORIAL OFFICE

*Measure: A Review of Formal Poetry*
Department of Creative Writing
University of Evansville
1800 Lincoln Avenue
Evansville, IN 47722

PUBLICATION

*Measure: A Review of Formal Poetry* is published twice each year.

SUBSCRIPTIONS

One-year subscriptions (2 issues) are $18, two-year subscriptions (4 issues) are $34, and three-year subscriptions (6 issues) are $50. Current and back issues are available for $15 each at our website.

SUBMISSIONS

Please see our website for complete submission guidelines.

WEBSITE

*measurepress.com/measure/*

SUPPORT

Funding for *Measure* is provided by a generous grant from the Ball Brothers Foundation of Muncie, from the Venture Fund, a program administered by the Independent Colleges of Indiana (ICI) for the benefit of Indiana's independent colleges and universities. Additional funding and support is provided by the University of Evansville. We would like to express our sincere appreciation to both organizations without whom this publication would not be possible.

COPYRIGHT

2013 by *Measure: A Review of Formal Poetry*

ISSN
ISBN-10
ISBN-13

1555-4791
1-939574-08-0
978-1-939574-08-4

# CONTENTS


EDITORS' NOTE     vii

| | | |
|---|---|---|
| *Turning Over a New Leaf* | Dick Allen | 1 |
| *Camera Obscura* | Bruce Bond | 2 |
| *In the Village of Berwyn* | James Matthew Wilson | 3 |
| *The Penitent* | Richard Meyer | 4 |
| *October Closing* | Richard Meyer | 5 |
| *Gout* | Sydney Lea | 6 |
| *Family Ways* | Susan McLean | 7 |
| *Getting One's Wordsworth at Henley* | Lewis Turco | 8 |
| *Mid-Bronx, 8 AM* | Lee Slonimsky | 9 |
| *Hamlen Brook* | Richard Wilbur | 10 |
| Wilbur's Intricate Simplicity | Roy Scheele | 11 |
| *The Walna Scar Road* | Michael Spence | 15 |
| *The Pumpkin Tower* | Michael Spence | 19 |
| *Daphne* | Michael Spence | 21 |
| *A Disaster* | Jeff Holt | 24 |
| *Elizabeth Barton's Last Reflections* | David Landrum | 25 |
| *My Date with Susan Calvin* | David Landrum | 27 |
| *Saints and Sinners* | David Landrum | 29 |
| *The View from Mars* | James Cotton | 30 |
| *Double Features* | Stephen Kampa | 35 |
| *Antaeus* | Mark S. Bauer | 36 |
| *Lament for Hector* | Mark S. Bauer | 40 |
| *Frozen Charlotte* | Susan de Sola | 43 |
| *The Finding-Again* (Translated by Donald Mace Williams) | Johann Wolfgang von Goethe | 44 |
| *The Return of the King Screens at Midnight at the Multiplex* | Maryann Corbett | 46 |

2013 X.J. KENNEDY PARODY AWARDS, JUDGED BY R.S. GWYNN

| | | |
|---|---|---|
| *Sonnet 130a* | Alan Nordstrom | 48 |
| *Museum Peace* | John M. Ridland | 49 |
| *This Be Much Worse* | Kathleen Naureckas | 50 |
| *John Donne, to the Kitchen of a Seafood Restaurant after a Forty-five Minute Wait* | Jack Borrebach | 51 |
| *Stop for Death* | Martin J. Levine | 52 |

| | | |
|---|---|---|
| *Entanglement* | Matthew Westbrook | 53 |
| *Thaw* | Joseph J. Capista | 56 |
| *Ninety-Six* | Joseph J. Capista | 58 |
| *The Choice* | Joseph J. Capista | 59 |
| *Eden's Serpent in Vegas* | Annabelle Moseley | 60 |
| *In the Harvest Moon* | Bob Watts | 61 |
| *Common Duties* | Bob Watts | 62 |
| *Matchbook* | David Stephenson | 63 |
| *For Halloween* | Austin Allen | 64 |
| *The Constant Moons* | Austin Allen | 65 |
| *Arachne* | Shangrila Willy | 68 |
| *Homework* | Rosanna Oh | 70 |
| *Waiting for Help* | Rosanna Oh | 71 |
| *Juno and the Paycock* | Peter Swanson | 72 |
| *North by Northwest* | Peter Swanson | 73 |
| *La Llorona* | Jack Granath | 74 |
| *The Flooded Grave* | Katie Hartsock | 76 |
| *Sestina in Memoriam* | Cindy Hill | 77 |
| *I Could Have Been Somebody* | Gretchen Hodgin | 79 |
| *A Novice Contemplates the Still Life* | Jennifer Fandel | 80 |
| *The Old Monk Undresses for Bed* | James Dempsey | 81 |
| *Hansel and Gretel* | Chris Bullard | 82 |
| *Fairest* | Alesia Thone Hill | 83 |
| *California Romance* | Michael Pearce | 84 |
| *Case Hardened* | Mark Blaeuer | 85 |
| *Eurydice Variation 7* | Kathryn Hinds | 86 |
| *The Gift* | Sherraine Pate Williams | 87 |
| *Red, Red, Red* | Rick Mullin | 88 |
| *King Lear* | Joseph Harrison | 89 |
| *The Quality Control Inspector's Last Day* | Christine DeSimone | 90 |
| *The Bourgeois Lover States His Case* | David Leightty | 91 |
| *Talking in Bed* | Philip Larkin | 92 |
| Unique Distances:<br>    On Larkin's "Talking in Bed" | Jehanne Dubrow | 93 |
| **BOOK REPRINTS** | | |
| *My Guardian Biped* | Gilbert Allen | 99 |
| *"Officials Are Optimistic<br>    He Has Been Killed"* | Gilbert Allen | 101 |
| *Daughter* | Gilbert Allen | 102 |
| *From an Athlete Dying Young* | Gilbert Allen | 103 |
| *Oklahoma* | Erica Dawson | 104 |
| *Back Matter* | Erica Dawson | 106 |
| *Intermission* | Erica Dawson | 109 |

*Little Black Boy Heads*     Erica Dawson     111
*Pomegranate*     Amy Glynn     112
*Dandelion*     Amy Glynn     115
*Chamise*     Amy Glynn     117
*Blackberry*     Amy Glynn     119
*Dogwatch*     R.S. Gwynn     121
*God's Secretary*     R.S. Gwynn     122
*Casus Belli*     R.S. Gwynn     123
*Victor Hugo: So Boaz Slept*     R.S. Gwynn     124
*Pedestrian*     Len Krisak     128
*Foyer*     Len Krisak     129
*Fit for a Runner*     Len Krisak     130
*An Italianate Façade on the Boston Garden*     Len Krisak     131

ACKNOWLEDGMENTS     134

CONTRIBUTORS     135

THE 2014 HOWARD NEMEROV SONNET AWARD     142

THE 2014 RICHARD WILBUR BOOK AWARD     143

THE TENTH ANNUAL ANTHONY HECHT POETRY PRIZE     144

# Editors' Note

At the Sewanee Writers' Conference this year, we had a chance during an editors' panel to remark on the abundance of good formal poetry being written and submitted to *Measure*. And then we asked for more of the same to come across our desk. As we approach the tenth year of publishing *Measure*, one thing that has been clear from the beginning is even more heartening now: the intelligent, innovative, varied, and informed use of meter and rhyme is alive and well. In issue after issue, we see poets of excellent, long-standing reputation alongside new ones, a mixture we have encouraged all along.

Another development seems to be a growing familiarity with meter and form even among poets who might not identify themselves as "formal poets." In fact, we often receive submissions from poets who do not write exclusively in meter and form, and that dexterity with both formal and free verse is good for poetry in general, demonstrating the expressive nature of metrical poetry and its ability to contain so many voices.

We would also like to issue a call for interviews of poets of note. Contributing Editor William Baer, as our subscribers and readers know, has supplied us with excellent interviews of notable poets from the beginning, starting with R.S. Gwynn in the first issue; but we would love to see a variety of voices and perspectives in our future issues.

Once again we would like to thank Contributing Editors William Baer and Katie Mullins; our administrative assistant Katherine Martyn; and interns Joy Grace Chen, Emily Krieble, Anna Sheffer, and Rachel Wyatt for their excellent help. And thank you for your support. We hope you enjoy.

Rob Griffith
Paul Bone

## Dick Allen

# *Turning Over a New Leaf*

Few things seem easier. Holding the page or maple leaf
Steady under your thumb, you slide your fingers
Beneath its thinness, then lift, then flip it quickly
Or let it reverse swan-dive like a swimmer
Clowning around on a diving board. And there
You have it, a totally new side — veined strangely
Or mottled, or carved with hieroglyphics,
Perhaps even blank and shiny. The possibility
Is anything can happen now: a single gust of wind,
A hurricane, one pen stroke or a whole book,
A whistle or a symphony. What lies ahead
Demands there must be nothing you hold back,
The leaf deceptively light, the light revealing
Almost at once what comes of such light turning.

# BRUCE BOND

## *Camera Obscura*

In my worst dream I am buried alive.
I go to work, to market, I chatter even,
though I barely hear the words that leave
my tongue, barely know the hearts that listen.
I could be falling asleep right now. Hell,
no one would be wiser. In my worst dream
I am a camera obscura with a needle
of light in the far wall of this, my room.
Think outside the chamber, says the sky
that neither does what it imagines nor knows
how tough, how strange it is to think inside.
Some caskets open as the eyelids close.
Each window a tunnel, each sky an echo,
each sun a shovel driven into shadow.

JAMES MATTHEW WILSON

# *In the Village of Berwyn*

My hands throb, stripped and ruddy with the winter.
Along the back fence, deer have crept at night
To crop our evergreens down to starved centers,
Until my futile bark sets them in flight,
    Their bright legs flitting out in the neighboring park.
    I turn, and shut the door against the dark.

The hallway boards are whited, smeared with salt.
Puffed boots, kicked off, lie soaking with wet socks.
The children whisper, shift in bed, then halt,
Halt at the slow creak of their father's walk.
    They listen, and I hear them listen there,
    For where I go, for what my hands may bear.

# Richard Meyer

## *The Penitent*

I tied a cincture round my heart
and cloistered it a world away
where it was humbled night and day,
a wizened little monk in gray.

But it was willful from the start
and spurned the halo-tonsured head,
the coarse unbuttered daily bread,
the lonely, cold, and narrow bed.

At length it could not play the part
and shed the cowl and sackcloth shirt
to feel again the thrill and hurt
of flesh and breath and sweat and dirt.

# RICHARD MEYER

## *October Closing*

The red and yellow tents come down,
the trapeze sky turns gray,
a lagging harlequin in brown
looks back and walks away.

## SYDNEY LEA

# *Gout*

He'd stood by the pond on that early-winter morning,
The ice all new, the new snow lying on
The surface. He felt himself acknowledging
The gallop of time, of course, but also warmed
To the notion of repetition: another year,
Another gilding of things by natural wonder,
And he a more than lucky witness there.
He stood again, this time in his living room, later,
And suffered a stab through his foot as if from a knife —
Or no, more surprising, as if from a nail mis-driven.
He hopped to a chair, but for hours felt no relief,
So at last, reluctantly, he traveled downriver,
Good wife at the wheel, to the clinic, where he would wait
More hours until the doctor announced, *It's gout.*

Something for portly old men at their port, he figured,
From accounts he'd read of the Tory poets, unlike
His own condition, at which he'd felt such pleasure
That very dawn: he'd been vain of the grueling hikes
He still could take despite his seven decades.
Early next morning he woke, as though not a thing
Had happened, and plunged into woods again as he had
For God knows how many mornings now, noticing
That the fog of last evening had frozen into lace
On each tree in the forest, its every branch aglitter,
Brilliant as gemstone. It was almost as if he'd lost
The very idea of discomfort, not to mention disaster,
Though he's heard what the weather report for tomorrow predicts:
Snow and rain at once, a nasty mix.

SUSAN MCLEAN

# *Family Ways*

A man who liked to have his way
        (and who does not?)
was keen to have the final say.
His sisters' tongues had lashed him raw,
so in *his* home his word was law.
Dissension was a fatal flaw,
        or so he thought.

A woman who desired a choice
        (and who does not?)
played dumb until she lost her voice.
Going along with his caprice
would quickly make the conflict cease.
What mattered was to keep the peace,
        or so she thought.

A child who wanted to be heard
        (and who does not?)
learned early on that mum's the word.
With no recourse but to comply,
her options were to sulk or lie.
She had her fill of humble pie,
        and so she fought.

Each of them fixed in their belief
        (and who is not?)
they dance their allemande of grief.
Still passing blame they each refuse,
they cannot wear each other's shoes
or change the steps. And so they lose
        the peace they sought.

Lewis Turco

# Getting One's Wordsworth at Henley

*A tailgater bluesanelle*

*I wandered lonely as a cloud,*
Sad, forsaken as a cloud.
My nose was bloodied but unbowed.

I had abrasions and a mouse,
A black eye bigger than a mouse.
I wandered lonely as a cloud

Over country lane and moor —
I looked like a demolished Moor;
My nose was bloodied but unbowed

Unlike my head, which was a mess:
Broken nose, a mouse: a mess —
I wandered lonely as a cloud,

Looking for a friendly mist,
The sympathy that I much missed.
My nose was bloodied but unbowed,

*I have not winced or cried aloud*
(Although I whimpered). I was proud,
Bewildered as a lonely cloud,
My nose still bleeding but unbowed.

## Lee Slonimsky

# *Mid-Bronx, 8 AM*

Who knows when "happy" first became a verb?
I do recall the first place that I heard
it used this way: a crowded subway car,
mid-Bronx, mid-May. A teen addressed his love,
"you happy me," caressing her red hair
at one of those mysterious long stops
in tunnel blackness. Braiding her hair in loops,
he kissed her then, as if to prove
his passion knew few bounds. Then lights went out —
a louder kiss — the train rolled slightly back —
some PA static roared, wordless. No doubt,
a rush hour crowd like this, heading to work
was not about to panic. Then we heard
an older woman's voice, almost a shout:
"Train, happy us and move!" So language spreads.

# RICHARD WILBUR

## *Hamlen Brook*

At the alder-darkened brink
Where the stream slows to a lucid jet
I lean to the water, dinting its top with sweat,
And see, before I can drink,

A startled inchling trout
Of spotted near-transparency,
Trawling a shadow solider than he.
He swerves now, darting out

To where, in a flicked slew
Of sparks and glittering silt, he weaves
Through stream-bed rocks, disturbing foundered leaves,
And butts then out of view

Beneath a sliding glass
Crazed by the skimming of a brace
Of burnished dragon-flies across its face,
In which deep cloudlets pass

And a white precipice
Of mirrored birch-trees plunges down
Toward where the azures of the zenith drown.
How shall I drink all this?

Joy's trick is to supply
Dry lips with what can cool and slake,
Leaving them dumbstruck also with an ache
Nothing can satisfy.

## Roy Scheele

# *Wilbur's Intricate Simplicity*

*"How shall I drink all this?"*
        *— "Hamlen Brook" (Wilbur 115)*

Richard Wilbur's "Hamlen Brook" is a six-stanza lyrical poem that explores the relationship of appearance and reality. At the outset the speaker appears to be a kind of Narcissus figure, bending over the brook's surface for a drink. But the poem quickly focuses on what he sees in the stream and reflected on its surface; rather than dwelling on the solipsistic, the speaker sees beyond self to the rich multiplicity of the natural world around him. This world is real to the speaker. In the "inchling trout" he spots on the brook's bottom, he does not see an instance of Plato's Theory of the Forms but instead a reversal of Plato's metaphor: the trout, a "spotted near-transparency," is "Trawling a shadow solider than he." As the reader proceeds through the poem, the sharpness and multiplicity of detail enter the argument on the side of reality, of the world as it is, bright and beckoning. The poet implicitly rejects a static world of eternal, perfected form.

The tension between these two extremes is apparent as one moves from stanza to stanza. In the first stanza the speaker stoops to drink from the brook, "dinting its top with sweat." He is not, however, attracted by his own reflection; instead, in stanza two his attention is drawn to the fingerling trout whose shadow is "solider than he." In the third stanza the speaker's attention remains on the stream bottom as the darting fish throws off "sparks and glittering silt." Stanza four returns to the stream's surface, where "deep cloudlets" are reflected; and, in stanza five,

> . . . a white precipice
> Of mirrored birch-trees plunges down
> Toward where the azures of the zenith drown.

The first five stanzas, then, show a back-and-forth shift of focus between the brook's surface and its bottom, which we might schematize as follows:

```
Stanza 1 (top)                          st. 4 (top)
   \                                  /            \
    \ st. 2 (bottom) — st. 3 (bottom)/             \ st. 5 (bottom)
```

This shift of focus between earth and sky is reminiscent of the Gaia/Ouranos story familiar from Greek mythology. Here, it emphasizes the theme of divergence, of the gulf between appearance and reality, the ideal and the actual, and it does so in typical Wilbur fashion, inviting the reader to participate in the poem's argument by immersing him or her in its images and metaphors. But in a Wilbur poem even the least conspicuous vocabulary choices typically support the poem's meaning. One subtheme of this poem is the contrast between the active and inert, and this contrast is reflected in an almost exact balance between past and present participles (there are eight of the former and nine of the latter). One of these will serve to illustrate the poet's astonishing control of such elements. In the third stanza he employs the past participial adjective "foundered" as an epithet of "leaves." On a first reading the phrase is almost shocking in its blend of contrasting aspects: the lightness of the leaves now heavily submerged on the streambed as a result of having "foundered," a word entirely unexpected but exactly right in the context. The leaves are rendered as so many small sunken ships — a metaphor compressed into a single word. The present participles, on the other hand, behave much as expected, introducing participial phrases or occasionally serving as a gerund but more frequently as an adjective (for example, "glittering silt").

Wilbur also works out the theme by metrical means. The first stanza is irregular, hinting at a certain hesitancy on the part of the speaker. The quatrain consists of a four-stress trochaic line, followed by a nine-syllable second line in which an initial pyrrhic foot and a spondee mimic the sense (Whêre thê/stréam slóws/tô â lú/cîd jét); the third line is an irregular alexandrine, while the fourth line, like the first, contains seven syllables (but here scannable as two iambs and an anapest). The syllabic pattern is 7/9/12/7, with the syllabically identical first and fourth lines seeming to confirm the reader's expectation that the poem's stanzas will be enclosed.

This expectation is quietly shattered, however, by the comment that carries the first quatrain's momentum over into the second. As one glances through the text, this first long sentence keeps going all the way down through the third line of the next-to-last stanza. That stanza's final line simply asks, "How shall I drink all this?" as it posits the problem of how to internalize the data of the external world. In the final stanza the poet offers his *sententia* after deliberating on the subject. This stanza is the only enclosed quatrain in the poem; the previous five quatrains have spilled over into this summation, this final wisdom. If we look again at the poem's metrics, we see that they too contribute to this earned wisdom. They shape the lines like a funnel to this end. Following the irregular metrical features of the opening stanza, Wilbur establishes a regular stanzaic pattern, the lines containing 6, 8, 10 and 6 syllables, the meter mostly iambic with the occasional substitution of a trochee for an iamb in the first foot, as in

> Tráwlîng/â shá/dôw só/lîdér/thân hé

or of a pyrric-spondee combination at the end of a short line:

> Tô whére,/în â/flícked sléw . . .

Often the movement of a line imitates the sense, as in the first two lines of stanza five:

> Ând â white/précîpîce
> Ôf mír/rôred bírch-/trêes plún/gês dówn…

Here the meter recreates for the ear the visual phenomenon being described; the anapest/dactyl side by side create a rapid crescendo and fall, a "sound precipice," as it were. The reader's ear confirms what the poet sees.

The final stanza's wisdom, like the rest of the poem, is built on an intricate synthesis of sensory data. The balance and tensions earlier described now strike a poise in the body and the emotions:

> Joy's trick is to supply
> Dry lips with what can cool and slake,
> Leaving them dumbstruck also with an ache
> Nothing can satisfy.

The spillover rhyme of *supply/Dry*, the reticent pun of the silent *b* in "dumbstruck," the long-withheld enclosed quatrain achieved at last — such subtleties are the abundant hallmarks of Wilbur's poetry. It is much easier to miss them than dismiss them; only a fool would attempt the latter.

MICHAEL SPENCE

# *The Walna Scar Road*

*England, 1997*

It's more a scar
Than a road: a car

Runs out of blacktop
Half a mile up

The first incline.
We hike toward the mine

Where they excavate
Coniston slate.

Streaked like marble,
The stone is dull

Green — the color
Of American dollars —

Which lends a façade
Of grace to a broad

Range of banks.
I grab a chunk,

But it's too big,
Making my pack sag;

So I take a splinter
For a souvenir.

We climb a path
That takes our breath

As much from the heat
And placing our feet

On cracked and loose
Stones as from views

Of these crags. A flock
Of sheep like rocks

Growing fleece
Instead of moss

Won't move as we pass
Near by. The grass,

Though short and flat
As a welcome mat,

Is abundantly crowned
With dung: the ground

Looks as if a sack
Of marbles black

And glistening was poured
Along the borders

Of this trail. The slant
Steepens, and we pant

Louder — the only speech
Now in our reach.

*A walking tour,*
Said the brochure

Convincing us to take
This trip through the Lake

District. Sweat
Itches its wet

Course down my neck
As if called by the beck

Whose dry bed
We must cross. Our tread

Becomes slow;
The way grows

More broken — we pause
To honor the laws

Of gravity.
Hoping to see

Its peak around
Each new bend

For so long,
We think we're wrong

When we reach the crest
Of this road at last.

Two thousand feet
In the air, we shout

Our triumph and tightly
Embrace. I recite

"The World is Too Much
With Us."  Then we catch

Sight of a girl tossing
A pink plastic ring

For her dog. There's no pack
Or gear on her back —

She hiked all this way
Up just to play.

She waves as we begin
The long path down.

MICHAEL SPENCE

## *The Pumpkin Tower*

That day I wheeled my bus
Through a left-then-instant-
Right-hand turn, I saw
With amazement this place —
A domicile uprooted
From Burien or White Center,
The poorer end of this route.
The roof dark as needles
Of hemlocks, walls slightly
Lighter like lichen,
The small wooden house
Hunkered low as a mushroom
Among the columned edifici
Which lent the neighborhood
Of Magnolia (though the flower
Doesn't ever grow here
Naturally) the cachet
That only cliffs of cash
Confer. Its four conifers —
Growing close, ragged, thin
As mizzenmasts — poked
The sky like sticks in the eye
Of decorum, high above
The zoning laws. Bound
Together by a lattice
Of ladders and platforms, the trees
Became a tower. From the top
Of the tallest fir
A black flag flew:
A sort of Jolly Roger —
Its skull a pumpkin, crossbones

A pair of cornstalks.
The ensign for a ship
Of scarecrows? Did they hail
From the desiccated country
Of October? No man of straw
Could hoist such a sovereign pennant:
A Disunion Jack that snapped
With contempt at all the lawns
Scalped as though taking cues
From the felt of pool tables,
The dopey topiaries.
For this house sailed a green
Far from simple grass —
A roil of vines tangled
As snakes drowned the yard,
Leaves thrusting up
Like splashes made solid,
Splashes made by the pumpkins
Bobbing there — orange floats
Broken loose from a net
Gaudy and gigantic.
Climbing the tower's legs
Like Laocoön's, tendrils
Spiraled double helixes
Toward the dark flag
As if trying to realize
Its depicted apotheosis:
When a new dawn — its sun
Ribbed as a stout hull
And stuffed with seeds — will sail.

MICHAEL SPENCE

# *Daphne*

The glare and cultivated air
Of scorn the high school student sears

The driver with as he climbs aboard
Is harsh as a klieg light, geared

To leave an afterimage sharp
As the shank of some bad-ass perp.

It works. Daphne's so impressed
When the student struts on past,

She senses the worst thing for this prick
Is to look uncool to the girls in the back.

She floors the gas, making him grab
Wildly for a handrail. The job

Has trained this driver well: she keeps
Her gaze on the road, her grin behind her lips.

§

The dark suit entering her bus, the head
A white balloon that seems to float its owner
Slowly up the steps (as though it's painful
For the suit to travel among the dungarees
And housecoats), the lips cracking a slit
To demand a transfer,
                    and when she holds it out
The arm whipping in a windmill arc,

As if a sudden gust has thrust the rigid limb
To snatch it —
                        until the driver ceases to care
What stirs up such a personal tornado,
Wanting to pop that pale balloon, to yank
The transfer back and leave the arm to reap
The vacant air, until the driver learns to use
The fare box for a windbreak between the suit
And the transfer she now waves, her little banner.

§

*Good morning*, Daphne would say, smiling
As the shipyard worker got on. Every day
For a couple weeks, she said the same thing —
He never said a word.

And never looked at her, flashing his pass
Like a sheriff's badge as he steel-toed his way
To the seat right behind her: the only place
Her rearview was blind. It occurred

To Daphne maybe the morning wasn't good
Enough for him to call it that so early.
So she tried *Hellos* and *How are yous?* Like wood,
His face; his voice stilled

In the well of his throat. She quit her greetings,
Deciding to echo him — she wouldn't be surly
But just ignore him. The bell rang
One morning: she pulled

To the curb. None of the riders
Got off. At the hiss as she released the brake,
He sprang up: *I want this stop!* Aiming a stare

Wide-eyed as if stunned, she said: *You can talk!?*

§

Her mother always told her growing older
Had advantages. But she had doubted it —
How much wisdom came from gaining pain
And wrinkles, moving slower while time sped up?

When she drove buses, the most surprising thing
Was the noise: teenage boys loudly bragging
Or lying (who could tell?) about the other boys
They'd beaten up; teenage girls complaining

In shrill peeps how boys mistreated them;
Children squalling beside their fathers sitting
Rigid as idols from a dead religion.
Did the passengers need noise to make them real?

Had everyone gone deaf but her? She saw
The irony when she grew hard of hearing,
Though not enough to stop her ears. But the years
Taught her to turn up the fans as high as they'd go —

Their blades pureed and blended all to a blur.

# JEFF HOLT

## *A Disaster*

A brief discussion, then security
Like ants spring into view.
These suits have come for you.
Others will pack your things. For privacy.

You tried to tell them you could work much faster.
They stared, and you despaired.
You'd thought your boss had cared
When you were sick. She hissed you're a disaster.

All present shook your hand, wished you the best,
Their eyes like chips of ice.
Walking, you feel a vice
Gripping your gut: you've failed the final test.

Not knowing why, you drift between blank men
Out of a tomb you'll never haunt again.

DAVID LANDRUM

# *Elizabeth Barton's Last Reflections*

*Hanged, 1533, for the treason of denouncing
King Henry VIII's marriage to Ann Boleyn.*

I cannot see the sun. The sky is grey
with gloom and rain, clouds low, streets muddy, chill
upon me and upon the crowd that waits
to see my end. I was a prophetess —
or so they said and so I had believed.
I saw visions, denounced the King, and gave
a judgment on his life: that he would sit
forever in a fiery chair in hell.
The people loved me, so the King dared not
lift hands to harm me. Then the rumors came.
His men said I was not a maid and that
I was a madwoman. The people soon
despised me. My divine perfection fled
like a defeated army; left me to
the mercy of state. Questioned for days,
I finally admitted all my words
were my own making, what my counselors
had whispered in my ears. I who had sat
with Wolsey and had spoken with the King
was borne off to the Tower. It was there
that Thomas Cromwell turned my heart away
and I confessed my prophecies had been
untruths. This is the last morning I'll see.
I'll die on Tyburn gallows — I can hear
steps in hallway, turning of key
in my cell door and hear its hinges creak.
No visions come; no voice assures my soul
it shall see grace. No angel comforts me.
The cart is waiting, and the rope; the crowd
waiting to watch me die. I am bereft

of the divine spell that once lifted me
on wings so I could glimpse the starry edge
of Paradise. I step up on the cart.
They tie my hands and tie my skirts. I glimpse
Lord Cromwell give the hangman a gold coin
so he will tie the rope tight and will make
my death a quick one. So. And I will pass
at least with this one mercy. What I see
is my last vision — and, I deign, my best.

DAVID LANDRUM

# *My Date with Susan Calvin*

Miss Susan Calvin dressed retro — she was
from 1950 after all. She still said *robot*
not *android*, and she did not refer
to artificial intelligence. I heard
no *cyber* hyphenated terms from her.
Plain talk, like she was plain in womanhood,
came from her lips. She wore a light blue blouse,
black pencil skirt below her knees, made up
and coifed with everything in proper place.
Susan and I went to a bar. We talked:
causality, free will, robots, whether
choice can exist or is an empty form.
We touch on semiotics: traffic lights
at 4 a.m. flash red and green though no
cars stop to see their signal. Is this still
communication? Night passed as if words
could speed up time; of positronic brains,
morality coded in circuit breaks.
A *robopsychotherapist* — title
she wore, the three laws etched into her soul
like scripture:  Do no harm to human beings;
the other two mere variations on
the first. Did her reflection reach beyond
cold mental, wire ties of robotic forms?
The night wore on, and our dreams flew about;
Drinks, talk, and lazy feelings of romance
all complicated logic. She and I
cannot be quantified or finalized
in an equation's space. A law creates
more possibilities than its strictures
extinguish. I saw golden light reflect
in her red wine, in her black hair and eyes,

thought of the distant worlds where robots live
and serve and die, obeying the Three Laws.
I saw it in the darkness of her gaze.

DAVID LANDRUM

## Saints and Sinners

The frescos on church walls in Italy
flash lurid scenes of horned devils who grin
as they torment sinners with verve and glee —
a show of the dire consequence of sin.

Beside these, painted panels display saints
lined up in Heaven, faces calm, their hands
uplifted placidly in worship — frames
exulting those who followed God's commands.

Yet saints' pale faces portrayed in the gold
of Paradise suggest a different hell:
the serpent-whisper that seduced their souls,
blinded their sight against the luring spell

of pleasure, made them hate their very flesh,
stifle their bodies, beat down their desires,
die with no husband, die wifeless, childless
so they could stand in one of heaven's choirs

as isolated sterile entities,
sated with emptiness eternally.

JAMES COTTON

# *The View from Mars*

1

Old Smith, the last surviving son of Earth,
Looked out across the deserts of red Mars
Where, over the ruined horizon, his birth-
World was setting, among the brighter stars.
Despite her seas of ash, her cities in chars,
Great distance made her, like a flake of snow,
So soft and faint it seemed her final wars —
Which anyhow had happened long ago —
Had dwindled to an ember, fleetingly aglow.


2

Her muted light, descending, drew his mind
Away from wastelands at his windowsill
And back to her, the mother of his kind,
Back to his boyhood on its clover hill
Where Smith had never aged or fallen ill,
Within that opalescent sphere, the past,
Whose fixed persistence now and always will,
Like shadows after twilight falls, outlast
The very sun from which their lengthening was cast.


3

Here stood the farmhouse, like an outspread sail
When steadily with wind it guides the keel,
Is staunch, is broad, is tall, the dolphin trail
Spuming a wake of constellated zeal
As if a starry choir were seen to kneel
Before the flowing altar of the sea.
Old Smith's a boy of five. Under his heel

Pressed grass exhales a mower's memory,
The breath of April evenings, steeped in brevity.


4
The sun has set, but night has not yet come.
The drowsy lawn is blue. With end of day
Pale moths that found the daylight burdensome
Awake to go a dark and wandering way.
Now, on the threshold, calling him from play
His mother's voice arches over the lawn.
Warmth from the open door spreads its blonde ray
Across a swath of grass, paling with dawn.
He follows her beckoning within. That time is gone.


5
Gone, too, the farmhouse, its temple height,
Its hill of glossy green, its circling shade
Of boughs. Gone this beginning of the night,
And just beyond the western fence, the glade
Of fiery wildflowers, repousséed
With twilight to a vast and burning sun
That, had it stopped for him, he would've stayed.
Already the crickets, ticking, have begun
As sound and symbol that another day is done.


6
Now Earth has set, and now Old Smith recalls
This time and place, as if the boy of five
Had just awakened to these sterile walls
Where, they said, humanity would thrive
But where, sustained, it only stayed alive.
Their spacecraft came like rafts of refugees,

Survivors without hope, but hopes to survive.
While famine's flesh-worms bored in grim disease
Raking hot coals of war, they staked their colonies.


7

Not everyone, but those who could afford
The exodus, sold all they owned and fled.
Though astronauts had long ago explored
The rock and deemed it lifeless, Life, they said,
Once Earth was uninhabitable and dead,
Life might be engineered. So engineers
Began to plan the Martian watershed.
With the last mass extinctions, the last years,
They made their landfall on alien hemispheres.


8

For mother Mars, they said, was going earthwise.
Its vapor plants, new built, would terraform
The airless void, the void round with globed skies;
Then ice ravines would melt, and rivers warm
Till moisture-pregnant winds brought forth a storm
To nurse the earth-born seeds and make them rife.
Bees, thawed from cryogenic tombs, would swarm
Sweet almond blossoms. Man would take a wife
And all would prosper here in love and newfound life.


9

That was the dream. They dwelt in huddled pods.
Hopes waiting for their paradise to be
They forwent Earth's ways, forgot Earth's gods,
Earth's monuments razed from all memory
But Smith's, and even his grown miserly.

Airlocks kept them safe to say their prayers
Under the swirling dust of the galaxy
And the wan dwarf star's deadly solar flares.
The colonizers grew old, and dying left their heirs.


10
But what heirs, what generations of men?
Their genes selected for confined space,
Thin gravity, and rationed oxygen,
They had begun to shrink, to brood, to pace,
To cease to be a noble, upright race,
Evolved to something other, something small.
Smith lifts his head from the pillowcase,
Sitting up, hearing footsteps in the hall,
And like a long, dusk shadow, leans over them all.


11
As pagans once their genius origin
They waddle in to offer him a drink,
But he, not thirsty, refuses medicine.
He hardly notices their strange eyes blink
At him like parchment with a fading ink,
The script turned cryptic, a lost people's dreams;
As now he sees, over the planet's brink,
Dawn's hot spring, welling in condensed beams
Gleaming, like strands of new-blown glass, on lustrous streams.


12
Are they streams, wending through meadows, plush
With knolls of rolling barley grass and furze
Rippling in a breeze? Has Mars grown lush?
The hummingbird, navigating, whirrs

Over a nectar sea of lavenders
Under a breathing, sweet, celestial dome.
How suddenly a miracle occurs.
Just past the glass and insulating foam
He seems to hear a voice, beckoning him from home.


13
Rising from bed, he hobbles down the hall
Where, pausing momentarily, he stands
At the airlock. Yes, stands and doesn't fall.
Turning the great bolts with trembling hands
He opens the door to endless prairielands,
And now, with strength beyond his feeble years,
He steps — where once were only desert sands —
Barefoot on grass, and in the distance hears
His destiny, diminishes, and disappears.

Stephen Kampa

## *Double Features*

The classic movie channel sometimes plays a pair
Of films the same leads starred in (Rogers and Astaire,
Flynn and de Havilland), so musicals might morph
To hardboiled noir — fedora'd gunmen guard a wharf
And punctuate the mist with pulsing cigarettes —
Or bland romantic comedies might cede their place
To pirates pirouetting through their rigged-up sets,
And everywhere those same two stars stand face to face,

Enchanted or entrapped (depending on the ending)
By passion so commanding, *our* love seems worth mending,
Something commendable — we share their magnanimity,
Their scripted grace, if not in praxis, then by proximity —
And we ignore the more appropriate connection:
Like them, we went from costars warbling warm aubades
After the nights spent trumpeting our predilection
For *pas de deux*, or lovers passed over by the gods

Of pained adieux, to moll and conman giving phony
Names to the feds and free rein to their acrimony,
Or pirates with their cutlasses drawn . . . what troubled creatures
We are, who now suspect each other's double features
And let our programs (onetime classics rereleased
For TV) do our talking for us, framed in black
And white. Most nights we take our cues from them, not least
In how we sleep: for twice as long and back to back.

## Mark S. Bauer

# *Antaeus*

I. The Mountains

They gripped each other neck and waist,
undetachable in circles paced
sideways. Each feinted: in, low, for the knees.
Then Father pulled him close, his left arm squeezed
them chin to shoulder, necks crossed, crown to crown,
and forced him lower, slowly, toward the ground.

And then the stranger braced, pivoted, dug hard,
and levered Father skyward. Turning toward
us, he grinned. His greaves and buckle gleamed
in the harsh Moroccan sun. Aeons, it seemed,
passed. Then slowly he folded Father up
occiput to pubis like a crumpled cup.
Father flailed until his lungs collapsed.
Then came that awful spinal *snap*.

II. The City

This Woonasquatucket, iced, brown-foamed, emerging
from beneath the expressway berm, serves as home these days
no matter where I sleep. Kids in the neighborhood
shout, "Gollum!" and to them I must be an amazing

sight: skittering from clump to clump along the banks,
tube and tank trailing. *Sarcoid,* the doctors state,
then in low tones: *Stiff pipes for his young age,* or gravely:
*rubberized alveoli,* sometimes: *inspissation*

*of the fluid in the lungs,* or simply: *constricted*
*inspiration* and other things I overhear —
Perhaps that's where I learned smart words like "occiput"
and "buckle."  And perhaps that's why I travel near

the scrawny creek that bears this native, mighty name:
Sluiced, dammed, wrenched, waterwheeled, then lashed in place by granit
blocks, it snakes by vacant mills — a convenience
whose colors once, according to industrial plan,

ran vibrant violet, green, yellow, red depending
on the dyelot of the day. It now runs black,
absorbing even February's crystal sky —
a vein of India ink, its only hues refracted

from transient skeins of oil that break apart against
old tires, cinderblocks, and toppled ginkgos that
outgrew their accidental perches. Ginkgo, Friend!
Self-seeded, cultivated by the grimy action

of scant seasons, of slow years:  A soilless place,
a bird's bequest, a life lodged between slime-slick blocks:
you grew until your scrawny canopy outweighed
your naked roots. No soil: the residue that caulks

these listing walls is moss, soot, spume, decaying bits
of leaf and fast food packaging, the product of
adaptive respiration just as much as I.
All this is overlaid on urban bedrock dense enough

to undergird this slathered-on ecology:
the world askew, fast-forwarding at speed the inverse
of the water's depth. Ginkgo: refuge, friend:
Somehow it seems I breathe more deeply here within

arm's-length and easier still when snuffling, as I tend
to do, around your base — as if your roots could guide
me somewhere dark and pure and clear. This is how I travel:
on the hardpack, trunk to smooth-barked trunk beside

this throttled, stumbling stream. I find it swallowed
now and then by intersections laid akimbo
across its path; it vanishes beneath steel sheets
spread thick with macadam, planted with lamps, made into

city streets — the only evidence of what's
below, odd creaks with every passing car. I track
the river down bare streets unrolled in plats oblivious
to older thoroughfares. Searching still, I tack

down block by block of triple-deckers jammed against
the curb, drawn always down those streets less desolate:
a tree or two whose roots have cracked their concrete slab,
red berries on the tendrils of a bittersweet

entwined along a chainlink fence, an over-grown
then died-back vacant lot limp in a spent riot
of brown — hollow lupine stems, joe-pye-weed clumps
bowed down, and what were once goblets of phlox on tiny

roots and, scattered through all, cartons, hubcaps, needles,
and other domestic jetsam piled up on this shore.
I scurry through this umber archipelago
of the city's eyesores. Strangely, again I breathe more

easily among these gashes than the city's gleaming
permanence of concrete, asphalt, plateglass, steel.
This winter afternoon I pick my path between
the sidewalk snowpiles, coarse-crusted, soot-flecked, bejeweled

with turds. A steaming clod sinks slowly, burrowing
until it reaches cement; rivulets of melted snow
reticulate, seeking low ground. I follow them
to where the river re-emerges, grimly flowing.


III. Hospice

Why tell you this? Why waste my breath on words,
as if such tales could conjure up some sense
in my rude roots, my distance now — my ordered
death, disordered life, this partial penetrance?
O for a hero's death! The spectacle,
the crowd, the blithe surrender to some hapless
cause, the brute finality of it all,
if only for a few bruised apples.

Passed down sure-handed from antiquity,
the scam attracts. Instead, my lot: to fade
away in urban anonymity.
No hero's sweat-slicked flesh, no greaves, no blade.
Only these sharp-edged, simple words I wield,
prying at pavement cracks until they yield.

## Mark S. Bauer

# *Lament for Hector*

*After a frenetic Saturday morning of admissions
on the Veterans Hospital psych ward*

### I. Deïphobos

Andromache, look at my brother run —
My heart aches
to see him skitter pell-mell as if some puppeteer
were jerking hidden strings. Hear these Greeks jeer
while my brother makes
himself a fool out on this sun-
scorched plain. No Trojan could foresee
this — This is not what the Gods had planned!
    *To the victors go the writing of history.*
    *A man divided does not stand.*

Who are you, you shell of a man, scrambling around
our walls? All Troy looks on, aghast:
Even priapic, simple Paris didn't bring the shame
to Troy that you have! You, whose name
*held fast* for us the last
decade on this killing ground!
In death dealt toe-to-toe at least there's glory —
But now you'll die a fraud, afraid, outmanned.
    *To the brave go the writing of history.*
    *A man divided shall not stand.*

### II. Andromache

Deïphobos, you don't even care!
Look at your brother — How can you watch him die?
Look at Achilles — Look at him swagger!

You take him on — Go after that braggart!
But you — You'd rather my

husband bleed and bear
Troy's pride alone. But he can fight no more.
What will be left? Just a bloody streak of sand.
     *To the brutal go the writing of history.*
     *A man divided will not stand.*

My love, couldn't you have walked away?
You said when you and Ajax met
he'd knocked you down: Didn't you know
by then that things could only go
badly? Was our life some side-bet
played at dice, some subplot in your play?
Who is it you think will sing the story
of your exit: bloody, virile, grand?
     *To the living go the writing of history.*
     *A man divided dare not stand.*

III. Helen

Andromache, Deïphobos: he was not yours — nor was he mine.
With me, though Queen, I think he was bemused
by friendship: private, simple, innocent.
His heart was in his home, but still he went
to war ("Tragic — " …he'd whispered lest he be accused
of thinking war was more than benign
sport). It tore him from us as he knew it would —
He knew what kinship and what honor would demand.
     *To warriors go the writing of history.*
     *A man divided cannot stand.*

His public fall from public birth
still terrifies our Trojans: For their own puzzled lives they'd pleaded,
urging him on to more, most manly violence.
To banish all ambivalence
is what so desperately they needed.
They told themselves that as he turned so turned the earth
and that the hero's helmet would itself bring victory:
Such forces no unvisored vision can withstand.
     *To the simple go the writing of history.*
     *A man divided must not stand.*

Susan de Sola

# *Frozen Charlotte*

I am a doll of ivory bisque.
I was a girl, but was too bold.
To preen in silks, I dared to risk
the open sleigh. I don't grow old.
A girl of flesh who died of cold.

I froze while riding to the ball,
to end in ice and snowy pearls.
I thawed in kilns, a molded doll,
a pocket *vanitas* for girls.
My cheeks are flushed. I died of cold.

I float now in a child's bath,
my little mistress pushes me
from rim to rim, or to her mouth.
They've taken all my finery.
A doll's not flesh. I don't get cold.

I'm safe for play — no moving parts.
My price is small. I'm bought and sold.
I fortify their frozen hearts.
*I'm warmer now* — the story's told
on mountain roads. I died of cold.

*Note: A "Frozen Charlotte" was a widely popular 19th century doll depicting a frozen corpse. The Frozen Charlottes recalled several ballads, known throughout America and Canada, about a young woman who froze to death on the way to a county ball. The popularity of the ballads and the dolls marks the deep resonance the story had for North Americans.*

# Johann Wolfgang von Goethe

## *The Finding-Again*

*Westöstlicher Divan VIII, 39*

Can it be! Thou, star of clearness,
Once more to my heart held so!
Ah, the midnight of unnearness,
An abyss it is, a woe!
Yes, 'tis thou, O sweet, most cherished
Adversary of my joys!
Mindful of our grief, late perished,
I mistrust the present's poise.

When in deep primeval powers
Earth lay on his timeless heart,
God ordained the first of hours,
Joying in creation's art,
And his "Let there be!" resounded.
Then burst forth the darkest groan,
And the All with might unbounded
In reality was flown.

Light appeared on the horizon;
Darkness shyly left him so.
Elements, now, loose their ties on
Each the next, and quickly go.
Futilely and wildly dreaming,
Each one rushed to be apart,
Fixed, in boundless spaces' gleaming,
Having neither voice nor heart.

Hushed and barren was creation;
Lonely, for the first time, God.
Then he made dawn; from her station,
She, in pity, far abroad

For the suffering and the troubled
Hung her singing hues arrayed,
And again came love, redoubled,
To what, each from each, had fled.

And with hasty, zealous striving
Each seeks for itself its own,
Form and consciousness reviving
In their lives' once boundless zone.
Rashly or in moderation
Joined, let them grasp and cling.
Allah, rest from all creation —
Ours, now, be earth's fashioning.

Thus, on morning's new-red pinions,
To your lips was I propelled,
And night stamps the best of unions,
Firmly, thousandfold gold-sealed.
We alike on earth are meted
A surpassing joy and pain,
And no "Let there be," repeated,
Shall disjoin us again.

Translated by Donald Mace Williams

MARYANN CORBETT

# The Return of the King
## *Screens at Midnight at the Multiplex*

Across the atrium, the motley queue
hypes its excitement. Costumed, buzzed, and loud,
the Elves and Humans preen. The Gandalfs (two,

one white, one gray) trade grins. No one is bowed
with pain of sacred knowledge or bad knees.
Volutes of latex turn them furrow-browed,

not mythic lore or rune-carved prophecies.
A giggling Arwen fidgets with her hem.
I'm suspect too, lined up along with these —

I've draped the silk, beaded the diadem,
tricked out the RenFaire, garbed the teenage knights
for an Olde Worlde. I wouldn't take it from them,

though something flinches in me when the lights
lower us into dreamtime: It's the New
that holds these minds in fee, and the fabled rights

of bard and *makar, geste* and *fabliau,*
give place to rendering and CGI.
Whether a helmet's drawn from Sutton Hoo

or Homer's Greece, they do not ask. And I
am riven in the dark, remembering
how, long ago, I swore the only way

into these glamours was to learn to sing
in ancient grammar. Oh my misspent youth:
As well escape your life with imaging

as riddle through the words of some dead mouth.
Embrace the eye-candy, the landscape porn.
To hear the tale that salves the sting of truth,

settle. Be still, and watch the chasms burn.
Adore, and take the popcorn on your tongue.
*The lyf so long, the craft so short to lerne.*

Films end. Dim ramps conduct us toward the bars.
We blink at lighted posters of the stars.

## ALAN NORDSTROM

# *Sonnet 130a*

My master's breath itself is none too sweet
Since Ralegh taught him how to smoke a pipe,
And even I, his dog, who smells his feet
Must say no rotten meat's more rank or ripe.
About his mistress, though, while dark of hair
And hue, and less than dulcet in her tones,
It's she looks after me and gives me care
And, when there's roasted beef, saves me the bones.
While he's ink-stained and in his writing fit,
Muttering lines and tapping with his shoe,
There's nothing here for me to do but sit
Or sleep and hope she'll save me from my rue.
    But ah! Outside the door I hear her tread —
    Dark goddess come, then I'll be walked and fed.

# John M. Ridland

## *Museum Peace*

*After Richard Wilbur, "Museum Piece"*

The ill-bred partisans of Art
Patrol the galleries and snipe
At anyone who does not praise
Magritte for *Ce n'est pas une pipe.*

They snuff one, dozing down the wall,
Deposed in his funereal *chair.*
A melting Dali clock drips Time
On what's left of his parting hair.

How the world turns! Aunt Grace is there,
But sprained her ankle, whispering *Damn!*
Dali loved to *épater*
*Le bourgeois gentilhomme et dame.*

Samuel Sewall bought on spec
A Dali smeared with palette knife
To hang above his bed's headboard
And watch while rogering his wife.

# Kathleen Naureckas

## *This Be Much Worse*

They fuck you up, your girls and boys.
  They may not mean to, but they do.
They take your gifts of life and toys
  And then give nothing back to you.

Sure, you're the one who fucked them up,
  but you were fucked up first of all.
Your folks passed you the poisoned cup.
  It's gone on ever since the Fall.

You're stuck with children once you've had 'em.
  They're near but they're not always dear.
Cain disappointed his dad Adam
  and all three daughters let down Lear.

## JACK BORREBACH

# *John Donne, to the Kitchen*
# *of a Seafood Restaurant*
# *after a Forty-five Minute Wait*

Batter my carp, sea perch and cod; for you
As yet but balk, laze, shirk and misattend;
That I may dine at last, boil fry grease, and bend
Your stoves to bake, broil, char and make me stew.

I, like an unstirr'd trawl, tuna overdue,
Labour to await you, but Oh, to no end;
Sheila, your waitress to me, me should befriend,
But proves slack, and blew my drink order, too.

Yet deeply I hunger, and cannot cut bait,
So am unmoored upon your apathy;
Secure me, grill pike or braise that trout, or skate;
Plate that for me, or any thing, for I,
Except you fulfill me, never fish shall see,
Nor dinner taste, except you serve it me.

# Martin J. Levine

## *Stop for Death*

Because I could not stop for Death,
He said he'd stop for me,
But called to say that he was stuck
In traffic on Route 3.

He called again. "I'm lost," he said.
"My GPS is fried.
I think I passed a school because
I saw some kids outside.

"A setting sun, some gazing grain,
I'm really in a jam.
A cornice, maybe? Or a roof?
Do you know where I am?"

"Can't help you," I said, shivering.
(I wish I had dressed better.
If I had known I'd be this cold,
I would have worn a sweater.)

The time went by. I worked and played.
The whole thing was forgotten
And then he called again to say,
"I really do feel rotten

To leave you hanging there like that."
I told him not to worry.
"Relax and take your time," I said.
"I'm really in no hurry."

Matthew Westbrook

## *Entanglement*

By midnight she had promised to be out,
and midnight came an hour ago.
I hit a string of yellow lights
along Route 1, but nudge the gas

to slip past each. You press
your foot upon a nonexistent brake.
Past small motels, lost-hubcap stands,
a trailer park, a mostly unlit lot

of used cars up for auction, then a long
scrap-metal yard, the turn we recognize as ours
beyond the Exxon's glare. A mile
of trees again, and then our street.

We closed the deal two weeks before,
then rented back to let the owner clear
the rooms of all she had: piano, beds
and dressers, children . . .

Now, turning up the residential hill,
we watch the silhouettes of house and yard
take shape: the dormers jutting from the roof,
the massive maple on the northern side.

A car is at the curb — it's not her truck —
and for a moment I imagine that
a realtor will emerge, head bowed, to say
the sale is off, the place not ours.

That moment disappears. The next,
we're striding toward the porch, our hands

and fingers interlocked. I separate
the key from others on the chain

and we go in. A moonlit wooden floor,
an empty living room. A twist of wires
where once had been a chandelier (the one
she said she'd take). An unfamiliar quiet

over all, made deeper with each clack
and creak of footsteps (ours). Before we find
a light switch, there's patter on the stairs:
a cat descends, leans past the banister,

and pads in silence toward us. We whisper,
stepping soft, and move to check
the kitchen: glass-faced cabinets
cleaned out; refrigerator vacant, humming

like unconsciousness on life support,
its light revealing nothing there but light.
You motion toward the doorway, say with eyes
we ought to leave — and yet I lead

us to the stairs, breath held, and up we go.
The top floor hallway's dark: all four doors
closed. I put a hand around the first
glass knob, the one to open what had been

her room. Imagine her alone, dead still,
her ears on every sound we make, or else
oblivious, asleep. Or gone: behind
the plaster wall, an empty bed — or none.

My hand won't turn. Instead, we turn
ourselves, descend the narrow treads and out

the door, across the porch and lawn, as if
we aren't still there. As if we never were.

# Joseph J. Capista

## *Thaw*

All afternoon police unearth
the dead from roadside drifts of snow.
It happens like this every spring:
a motorist reports the tint
of darkness in a melting pile
or catches sunlight glinting off
a well-sewn button or a shoe.
Perhaps a hand, a bud unbloomed,
extends there toward imagined help.
Found are those whose orbit slipped
some imperceptible degree
before we ever thought them lost.
It seems like only yesterday
we watched a drifter stagger through
three lanes of traffic, arms asway,
as if conducting some rush-hour
*motet* his ears alone could hear.
He waved. I almost waved right back.
In lilac light the cruisers flashed
against the dusk as someone dug
while someone else rerouted cars;
we drove directly home where now
we lie together and converse
about these newly exhumed dead.
I know you fear our daughter woke
mid-fight this evening, woke to hear
about our own dissolving dreams,
about this falling in and out
of love. The dead are neutral ground
and so, exhausted, spent, to them
we steer our words. It's almost prayer.
Tonight they'll rise from depths inside

of me and pool behind my eyes
until their pressure rives my lids
and up they climb and float across
my mind's sky till they're gone for good.
I'll wake. The bedside time machine
will blink its 4:00, its 4:01.
And as I turn and drift once more
toward sleep, I'll think of them before
I slip my hand in yours. But first,
so that my touch won't startle you,
won't wake you from unquiet dreams,
I'll hold my hand out to the night
and let it grow a little cold.

JOSEPH J. CAPISTA

# *Ninety-Six*

My friends who went to art school were employed
in sundry funky undertakings, not
in office parks. They said, "You have a *choice*,

man: mind your mind, lest the man destroy
the choice you have." They often spoke like that.
My friends who went to art school were employed

as porno-movie extras, shoe-shine boys,
a lifeguard at a nudist camp abutt-
ing office parks. They said I had a *choice*,

perturbed I temped, took calls, greeted, read Freud
and Dante on the clock. Filled coffee pots.
My friends who went to art school were employed

as roadies, clowns, baristas whose soy
lattes and pierced lips were too taboo for suits
in office parks. They said they made a *choice*:

sniff crank, crank grunge, and mosh. At work I lied
and got a raise and quit. I now teach art.
My friends who went to art school are employed
in office parks. They have, they say, no choice.

## Joseph J. Capista

# *The Choice*

*Perfection of the life, or of the work*
*— W.B.Y.*

I only saw him once, the baker whose
pandoro, sfogliatelle, and anginetti
imbued the meat-thick deli air with sweet
aromas as they cooled in perfect rows
behind the register. I'd heard he pressed
each fingertip in salt, then pulled a stack
of trays — barehanded — from the oven's rack;
as such, this mitt-less artisan produced
his sweetmeats, saved from burn by callous.
*Psycho,* I hummed above the slicer's blade.
Who maims himself for pastry? And by choice?
Immersed in thought, I nicked my thumb. I bled.
To pack with salt or bind with stitch this wound:
the choice was mine. I chose what I could choose.

# Annabelle Moseley

## *Eden's Serpent in Vegas*

*"Now the serpent was the most cunning of all the animals..."*
— Genesis 3:1

Do you like cards? Let's play. Draw up a chair.
I always bite the Queen of Hearts for luck.
You see her dog-eared King there? What a pair.
Sometimes my spittle stays; I get them stuck
before I cut the deck, and you'll observe
they rarely end up in the same hand. Fold.
I almost always win. That's why you'll serve
me playing straight or cheating. Oh, it's old,
explaining how I know the Braille of lies —
twitch, scratch, the way the players move their hands.
I tell you that it isn't in the eyes.
Before you reach, I can predict your plans.
Desire trembles in the fingers first.
Your thumbs betray your longing. So, you're cursed.

This game is more than allegorical.
It's said that some can sense a coming rain
within their joints. My skin's an oracle
that way. I shed my memories, shed the pain
of all my patients, as I deal and bluff.
You can't imagine all the fools I've healed.
I'm told that my prescriptions can be tough.
I've always dealt out honesty, revealed
the truth, like with my infamous first play.
Speaking of rain, the garden was slick-wet
the day I whispered to her. To obey
without first tasting brings about regret.
She learned that from me. So did he. Death's small
compared to knowledge. Deal now. Touch me. Fall.

Bob Watts

# *In the Harvest Moon*

Blueberry child, or smaller still, a grain
of wheat, a poppy seed, already you
were sown in curving rows of DNA
with a crop of family traits to grow into.
Perhaps the bloom of your great-grandmother's smooth
and ageless skin, this uncle's long-limbed frame,
or that aunt's thatch of curls, some lost heirloom
of cheekbones found in a familiar face.

All we can know for sure is that you picked
your mother's inability to wait
for what she wants, your father's need to stay
a careful distance from the ones he loves,
the parts of us we didn't want to give
the qualities that carried you away.

## Bob Watts

# *Common Duties*

What can I call the quality
with which he did each thing he did —
coaxing an oak beyond the bias
of its long-limbed sunward lean,
or carving a log road up the hill
as someone else might peel an apple,
changing a diaper or a tire —
the two-toned polyester blue,
work-booted grace that made each task
a kind of prayer, unvoiced and endless?
I find the world harder to move,
or more, harder to move myself
through it without his certainty,
as casual as the baseball cap
he tilted back to mark the end
of work, his faith that any task
done well becomes its own reward.
Let it teach me the sacrament
of loving all I have to do,
show me the holiness in a line
of postholes dug sharp-edged and deep,
holy the green bean runners staked,
hay raked in snaking, sun-dried rows,
the bed sheet folded on its shelf,
the floor swept clean, and holy too
the words that move a fat red oak
to fall where it will be of use.

# DAVID STEPHENSON

## *Matchbook*

We twenty brethren formed up like a choir
Were born to feel sandpaper on the face
And burst into a handy ball of fire.
It is a destiny that we embrace.

1 through 3 went for a charcoal grill,
4 and 5 for big candles in jars,
6 and 7 to heat some scented oil,
8 through 10 for gas station cigars,

And so on, until now we three remain,
Seemingly forgotten in a drawer.
Our hearts have turned to stone, yet we maintain
Our focus, our commitment, our desire,

Our certainty that someday we'll be found
And stricken, and flare up, and burn down to
Some smoking ash and cinder, and go out
Having done what we were meant to do.

AUSTIN ALLEN

## *For Halloween*

Vodka blood punch, communion with the host
who is Paul Bunyan and already drunk;
two wolves, a wine-stained Roman and a ghost
whose tattered hem and silver-powdered breasts
and laughter seem to trail me all night, hovering —
I the nefarious, hairy Russian monk
still swallowing draughts of poison and recovering.

Petticoats! Tweeds and weaves! Baubles and bangles!
All clothes are pulled out of a flim-flam trunk.
Why don't more parties end with all the guests
circled by flashlight in their flesh and fur,
telling their stories with the rags torn off their chests?
That's what they seem to want. As I want her
over the bed, moon low, ghost linen at her ankles.

Austin Allen

# *The Constant Moons*

Out of Uranus,
out of the clear blue sky,
inside the inmost ring,
during a certain phase,

lighting a cigarette
(the atmosphere somehow
seems to allow it),
Universe, to you

I speak. Words plucked
from the galaxy's whorled ear.
Out of Uranus. Presto:
out of strange, thin air.

> *Exit Titania, exit Oberon,*
> *exit Miranda, Ariel, and Umbriel.*

Universe, I place my faith
in you. Where else?
Out of a secret pocket
in the bureaucracy of stars,

a loophole in the fabric,
you will manage to pluck —
on my behalf — a moon.
You'll pull some strings.

I will seize the trailing locks
of opportunity's comet,
hightail away
astride a nebulous horse.

*Exit Cordelia, Ophelia, and Bianca.*
*Exit Cressida, Desdemona, and Juliet.*
*Exit Portia and Rosalind, pursued by Cupid.*
*Exit Belinda, Perdita, Puck, and Mab.*

Some distant night,
on some Plutonian shore
by a nitrogenous river,
all the dead shall meet,

and smoke, and act
much as they did before.
Drinking their green caipirinhas
on a moraine slope.

Or their twins will,
or the twins of their twins.
Only a little different,
under a Charon moon.

*Exit Francisco, exit Caliban,*
*exit Stephano, Trinculo, and Sycorax.*
*Exit tardy Margaret, hasty Prospero,*
*retrograde Setebos, distant Ferdinand.*

Exeunt omnes.
Goodnight, moons.
Goodnight, you sinking gods
and dwindling men.

Into the curtsy
of gravity you dip,
sweet ladies. Goodnight.
Until we meet again.

My cigarette dwindles
in a nice slow burn.
Goodnight. You've all
been lovely. Until soon.

> *Silence a while, then a stirring within.*
> *Enter Titania rising in her turn.*

## Shangrila Willy

# *Arachne*

That unkempt summer, she watched them spin
their filmy webs across the limbs
of the beech, tough filament as thin

as fingers, flickering in the dim
at their appointed hour. Soon,
she'd learned their knack for silk, and prim

as any orb-weaver, she loomed
her heart-spun yarn into the weft
of tapestries where children bloomed,

round-fingered, rosy-cheeked, a deft
suggestion of golden curl. Her fame
increased, as in relief, the heft

of it rising from the wan, white plain
of her day, which carved for her a throne
from nothing. When Athena came

to challenge her, she was only bone
and pride, a fierce, venomous bite
distilled by her dwindled size, her own

concoction, born of sleepless nights,
within the empty room she bore.
She wove a catalog of spite:

the gods as careless wastrels, more
animal than divine — true lies
as she saw it. Athena swore

revenge and gave her eight black eyes
that multiplied the fractured world
into a ceaseless, sharp reprise

as every morning she unfurls
her tragedy in sticky thread,
a graceful elegy of whorled

insanity that she must shred
and eat before she goes to bed.

# Rosanna Oh

## *Homework*

> *"Your homework was to describe where you live. And unless*
> *I'm mistaken, you do not live in a 'great house cherished by*
> *the gods,' but over your mother's grocery shop."*
> — *Angel's schoolteacher,* Angel *(2007)*

I wrote in Mrs. Katz's fifth-grade class
in Jericho, Long Island, this short answer
for homework: "It's been busy for the past
few weeks at home because of Yom Kippur.
I stay behind the register to bag
the groceries. My dad wakes up at one
to buy fish in the Bronx. Sometimes I gag
if he smells bad. When Mom's store chores are done,
her hands feel rough from rose thorns and steel wool."

I got a check-plus-plus for my concreteness.
The teacher wrote in red, "Your friends at school
can learn from you. Present this after recess."
So I obeyed. A boy's laugh cut me through.
Should I pretend my stories are untrue?

# ROSANNA OH

## *Waiting for Help*

We're stuck on Brooklyn Bridge. It's New Year's Eve.
My son wants Dad and Jane. Behind our car,
an ambulance wails, urging me to grieve.

I honk. The kid starts tugging at my sleeve
then yells, "ARE WE THERE YET?!" into my ear.
"We're stuck on Brooklyn Bridge! It's New Year's Eve!

What do you think? Why can't your father leave
his perfect house to pick you up?" Somewhere
an ambulance wails, urging me to grieve.

My son prefers his stepmom, my pet peeve.
I wonder how I've made it here, so far:
we're stuck on Brooklyn Bridge; it's New Year's Eve;

the kid boasts of the presents he'll receive
this evening — *Call of Duty, God of War.*
An ambulance wails, urging me to grieve.

On holidays, my ghosts all interweave.
News of a shooting comes on NPR.
We're stuck on Brooklyn Bridge. It's New Year's Eve.
An ambulance wails, urging me to grieve.

## PETER SWANSON

# *Juno and the Paycock*

The sinners line up at the nearest bar.
The mother of our God keeps candles lit
And even though there's knocking at the door,
And in her heart, she will not answer it.

Men test the sea in hopes of being drowned
Or go to war to feel the bullet's knock.
And daughters lift their skirts to men who grind
Their way from pub to alleyway to dock.

And mothers weep, and still believe in God,
And set their jaws against the sudden turn,
The light gone out, the deep sea's cold,

The bloodied boy, the whiskey-buying bawd,
The swollen girl, stupidity of man,
And hearts of flesh that turn to hearts of stone.

PETER SWANSON

## _North by Northwest_

Think thin, America, in silhouettes
Of evening dress and city lines.
Think what the fashion of your money gets —
It buys your architecture and your signs.

It buys the structure of your cocktails,
And single-breasted suits in gray,
And girls with all the right details.
It buys you clever things to say.

And in dark bars and railway cars,
When the light is dim enough, the gin
Just cold enough, the girls American

And tall and blonde enough, one hears
The torch song and not the prehistoric wind
That's always sweeping down the plains.

## Jack Granath

# *La Llorona*

And La Llorona's vision of the future,
Often mistaken for a memory,
Drops from the tongue of yet another teller:
Two children taken to the water's edge
And drowned. The one who does it is their mother.
The reason — madness, evil — doesn't matter;
What does is the explosion of regret
She knows at once, the slap of those cold waves,
And her eternity of mourning. Night —
Night after night she roams that shore and wails.

Good storytellers understand the weight
Of those four syllables, *eternity*,
But not in a religious way. Deep down
They've always known the late philosophy,
That given an infinity of time,
Each piece of dust that makes us and our world
Must recombine in this exact display
And we live out our lives again, come back
Eternally to every particle
Of pain that we feel now. And this is what
The woman in the legend wails about.

But others understand it differently,
This folklore-fairytale eternity.
Infinite space negates that little game.
Our broken parts will not combine again
If traveling in opposite directions.
But still, is that supposed to solace us,
The universe as endless field of loss?
One woman's pain may end but only thanks
To the annihilation of all things.

Is that what this new teller tries to say,
This grandma tucking in the restless kids?
One of them weeps and wants to know the names
Of the two children who had died like that.
She gives the question lots of thought as if
Remembering and suddenly decides
To tell them La Tierra and El Aire.
These are the words that La Llorona wails.
For now they are — until there comes another.

## KATIE HARTSOCK

# *The Flooded Grave*

*— after the light box by Jeff Wall*
*Art Institute, Chicago*

Beside the shoveled mound of lea,
a red-orange-yellow shoal
of starfish and anemones
dwells within the hole.
Far afield, a hose lies flat,
pointed at this pool
as if its shower gave the *fiat*
*lux.* Gravediggers' tools
can resurrect, the burial
ground can learn to swim.
Walled in by earth, germs of tidal
foam still top the scrim
of cropped saltwater. Visions prove
how they live: they move.

KATIE HARTSOCK

## CINDY HILL

# *Sestina in Memoriam*

I loved to watch my great-grandmother fold
and roll and cut holes in the old newspaper;
scissored snowflake held across her face
as if it were a piece of Spanish lace
or silken veils swirling through her hands
as she waltzed across the floor, and not

some bakery string shoved in a drawer in knots
or some small orphaned bird she would enfold
and hold until it died in tender hands,
then bury wrapped in scraps of colored paper
tied in tattered shreds of hoarded lace
beneath the lilac bush, tears on her face.

There's nothing that tough woman couldn't face:
no siblings' quarrel, tangled lovers' knot;
no child born outside of bridal lace;
no piece of laundry that she couldn't fold;
no choice she could not diagram on paper,
thinking not with mind, but with her hands.

I loved to watch my great-grandmother's hands
in mock-drama dismay rise to her face
at something cynical in Sunday's paper;
or as they eased a wide comb through the knots
of my long auburn hair, then braid and fold
and tie it with a bow of fresh white lace.

She stitched her wounds at home, saved old shoelaces,
sewed money into petticoats by hand.
Inside worn flannel shirts, she'd hide her billfold
but look the auctioneer straight in the face —

her purchase strategies a Gordian knot —
She said that they made sense on ledger paper.

I loved to watch the way she fashioned paper
dolls, lined old steel cupboard shelves with lace,
coiled silver hair in perfect knots
each day, and even when her aching hands
could barely grasp the soap, she'd wash her face
each night, then clasp her beads in prayerful fold.

Her name is written on a paper card held in my hands,
bordered with black knots, embossed with crosses of black lace.
Let me be the one to fold the cloth over her face.

## GRETCHEN HODGIN

# *I Could Have Been Somebody*

*"The woods are lovely, dark, and deep,*
*But I have promises to keep."*
*— Robert Frost*

When people ask me what I'm working on,
I say the pole. If that were true I'd pay
my rent. Unlike the Cinderella heels
and walls, the ceilings there aren't made of glass.
It's this exotic promised land where blondes
make bank off adolescent years of dance.
And here I've wasted tap, piano, jazz
(my rhythm!) on thin white lines that I support
with credit cards, and selling shit on Ebay.
I'm telling you, I've got some sick-good moves,
and nothing's sexier than keeping beat.
They'd put my face on posters smacked against
the doors and call me Madame Asserfly.
Damn, I'd be rolling in a Lexus now.
Ironically, I'm here in front of some dude
I've never seen (and on my knees, no less).
I say, *Alright, I guess you really are*
*my shepherd; I will not want to take a class*
*on firearms, or gorge myself on Lexapro,*
then mutter to myself another psalm:
*I still have shit to do before I die.*
*I still have shit to do before I die.*

JENNIFER FANDEL

## *A Novice Contemplates the Still Life*

My body stiff against this hard-backed chair,
I dream beyond this scene of simple lust
where I pretend the food's not gone to dust
and cellar mold's not thickening this damp air.
But if a woman's footsteps creaked my stairs,
I could toss high this bread's old, ragged crust
and do the honor of sculpting her bust
or paint her nude with a forgiving stare.

Although I can't quite master brazen skills
convincing ladies of my honest art,
desire's arranged on today's windowsill
as wine, a bread loaf, an orange torn apart.
And that passers-by may think what they will
I eat fine oysters and artichoke hearts.

JAMES DEMPSEY

# *The Old Monk Undresses for Bed*

Gentle Jesus, if I may,
I offer you this dying day
That dangles darkly in the trees
And closes like clogged arteries.
I also offer, Lord, to thee
My nightly glass of J&B
And laud the joy it doth impart
To the red muscle of my heart.
From my belly I unwind
My rosary, in which men find
That long concatenation of
Your mother's weal and woe and love.
I doff my alb and scapula
Take off my Saint Jude medal, a
Present from mother, may she rest
In peace upon Your Father's breast.

The boxers fall, off comes the shirt;
Nude as a babe and old as dirt
Here stands the sinner in his sin
With floppy dugs and dry, loose skin
And sadly hanging urinator.
Apologies, my poor Creator
for what my body has become.
And now I lay my holy bum
And all my yet-uncoffined meat
Upon this white, forgiving sheet.

## CHRIS BULLARD

# *Hansel and Gretel*

The old wife cackled, "Please, come in."
Was she a witch? Why should they care?
They were too starved to imagine
She hungered, too. Perhaps, she'd share
Potatoes roasted inside their skin
Or marrow bone soup with Gruyère.
The old wife cackled, "Please, come in."
Was she a witch? Why should they care?
Then she was dead. *Man muss essen.*
They baked her for their daily fare.
Soon, that bony cupboard was bare.
Next door at another cabin
An old wife cackled, "Please come in."
Was *she* a witch? Why should they care?

## ALESIA THONE HILL

# *Fairest*

Dried petals in a bath fade into white
as they rejuvenate. Spirits adrift,
they cling to porcelain, to slender feet —
tangle in ashen curls, graze hips and wrists.
Lorraine envisions goldfish swimming around:
tails and fins grazing, and fish lips tasting
the fragrance left on her skin. The newly formed
petal-fish swarm around her in dizzying bubbles
until she cannot watch them anymore.

Her bridesmaids later marvel, pin her hair back,
paint her nails. They swirl, and swirl, and swirl —
bathe her in compliments, pressing close.

## MICHAEL PEARCE

# *California Romance*

We met in Calaveras
on a dry creek bed
I wore a tan fedora
you were dressed in red.

We kissed in Yuba City
on a moonful night
I opened my eyes
yours were shut tight.

We robbed a store in Belmont
ate lunch in Burlingame
by the time we got to Lodi
you wouldn't speak my name.

You broke my heart in Red Bluff
I broke your nose in Weed
you told me I was evil
I just watched you bleed.

We'll meet again some day
after a great rain
I'll bring the killer
you bring the pain.

Mark Blaeuer

## *Case Hardened*

The smith, an *angry* man is he. Repeatedly,
he pounds hot, red-hot, iron. The anvil must allow
a raw debility (a line of fathers) to
shape the odd ornaments, gate latches, ox shoes, toys
forged, or attempted once, for a coal-spotted boy.
If there persists a comfort in this heated show,
he won't appreciate the irony of blow
and bellows yielding solace to cold memory.

The wife he's nearly killed through welding hate
to all things gentle isn't gone just yet.
She feels the old and new souls balancing
inside her body. *Never let the sting
of evil interfere with good*, she'll say.
She and her son, and nascent daughter, stay.

KATHRYN HINDS

# *Eurydice Variation 7*

Your lyre is flesh. When you are truly dead,
it will not sound: ghost fingers cannot pluck
those plangent, tangent strings. Still, with luck,
you may retain that vibrant voice that pled
so well for my release. Unlikely. Here
all words, all songs, lengthen and rise to wails
and moaned laments; your art may not avail
in this unpleasing place of deadened ears.
But when you cross the Styx, a fading man, you'll see
your fellow shadows reach impatiently
to pluck at you. Would you requite their plea?
Keep silence, watch and listen, then perchance
you'll learn; you cannot lead this time. Advance
with me: I have taught the shades to dance.

# Sherraine Pate Williams

## *The Gift*

What I remember most about that strange moment
as your car pulled away from the open hydrant
in front of what had always been, until then, your
house, too, was not the kid-rushing, gushing allure
of water spray, but the way you seemed so content,

as if the playful stream washed the scant years misspent
with us — my mother and me — away, down cracked cement
of suburban sidewalks, to drown us in a slum's gutter.
What I remember most

came later, in years without your smug, inconstant
swindler's face: the chip my shoulder grew, my penchant
for invention, the quick lies I learned to tell, sure
I, the throw-away, could camouflage your error.
But your blight reveals its value. I can't resent
what I remember most.

RICK MULLIN

## *Red, Red, Red*

I'm not supposed to be here at this hour,
lolling at the cluttered secretary,
early, late. I wasn't meant to feel
the sun surmount the hemlock row and tower
to where its light attains a sedentary
cast, a halting moment on the wheel
that holds the eye of heaven on that red
depression glass, the empty beaded vase.
I didn't notice I'd become a ghost,
a dusty shadow from an unmade bed
dissolving in a veil of seven rays.
Beholden to the moment and its host
of casualties, I wouldn't see this stain,
vermillion from the morning's open vein.

JOSEPH HARRISON

## King Lear

Of course some wise guy *would* nickname him "King,"
That Princeton rookie with his college ring
Pitching for Cincinnati, who finished last.
He couldn't hit, or run, or throw it fast,
And didn't binge or brawl or anything,
Just floated a knuckleball they swung right past.

A player's tale: the spotlight of renown
Switched off, you're yesterday's ticket, out of town
And back to Charles. He hurt his arm next year
And he was gone like luck, or penny beer.
And when an old man's mourners set him down
In wind and rain, who knew he was King Lear?

## CHRISTINE DESIMONE

# *The Quality Control Inspector's Last Day*

*— February 9, 2002*

The Japanese have a word, *Karōshi*,
for "death from overwork." That winter dawn,
he didn't have time for the breakfast she'd
prepared — *natto* soy beans, pickled *daikon*
radish. He had fourteen hours to make up
the eighty from the week before, so he rolled
from bed to do every task again, to take up
*ganbaru:* bear it without complaint. He'd told
his wife, *The moment I am happiest*
*is when I can sleep.* At 4AM, he slumped over.
Just thirty, they called it ischemic heart disease
but the baobab can go years without flower.
He could feel the slow rush of Mikawa Bay
as his heart found its happiness, sailed away.

David Leightty

## *The Bourgeois Lover States His Case*

We cruise home down a prim suburban street,
Unload the groceries, nuke some barbeque;
Coax kids through homework, baths, a bed-time treat.
Some nights there's even time for just us two.

It's true — I lack the cowboy attitudes
You loved in him — the thrills and, yes, the frights.
Then too, I lack those dark, conflicted moods
You hated, when he stormed out angry nights.

I cannot bear to think you might regret
Today the choice grief would not spare you, then.
Walk through our home; watch, aching with delight,
These sleeping children you'd have never met,
And tell me if you would not choose again
The earnest love that comes home every night.

David Leightty

PHILIP LARKIN

## Talking in Bed

Talking in bed ought to be easiest,
Lying together there goes back so far,
An emblem of two people being honest.

Yet more and more time passes silently.
Outside, the wind's incomplete unrest
Builds and disperses clouds about the sky,

And dark towns heap up on the horizon.
None of this cares for us. Nothing shows why
At this unique distance from isolation

It becomes still more difficult to find
Words at once true and kind,
Or not untrue and not unkind.

## JEHANNE DUBROW

# *Unique Distances:*
# *On Larkin's "Talking in Bed"*

I have argued with my husband. Or, rather, we've had the beginning of an argument that then became silence as he walked away from my voice to shut the bathroom door and take a shower. We are on vacation, a three-day drive from home, which means that the hotel room suddenly becomes the whole world. I cannot leave. Where would I go? Our dog sleeps on the bed. The miniature refrigerator hums in the cubby of a wood armoire, beneath a flat-screen TV. On the other side of the wall, I hear water splash on.

When my husband emerges from the bathroom, first in a towel, then in nothing, and then at last in his pajama bottoms, we do not speak. This could go on for hours. And later — or very soon — we will click off the bedside lamps, each of us pushing under the white covers, and we'll say nothing.

Philip Larkin must have known this scene when he wrote "Talking in Bed," which appears in his book *The Whitsun Weddings* (1964) and which describes any couple that has ignored the popular injunction: *never go to bed angry*. The title suggests we are about to read a poem that illustrates or explores the act of "talking in bed." The reader quickly learns the title is an abbreviation of the opening line and that, in fact, the poem examines the act of *not* talking. The tension between the expectation created by the title and the poem's narrative is the tension between what we want love to be and the blacked-out, angry room that love sometimes is.

"Talking in bed," the speaker begins, "ought to be easiest" (1). "Ought to" is shorthand for disappointment. We find the same "ought to" in Larkin's "Home Is So Sad": "A joyous shot at how things ought to be, / Long fallen wide" (7-8). "Ought to" is a synonym for the dropping off of expectation, the imperfection of people who desire contact but fail to connect nonetheless. The first tercet, then, explores what "ought to." To talk in bed with one's partner should be natural and effortless, because that closeness of two bodies lying together implies emotional closeness: "Lying together there goes back so far" (2). This phrase, "back so far," suggests that pairs have always lain like this. We could return to the cave and find Cro-Magnon couples in the same prone posture, able to speak their fears in the anonymity of night.

Of course, Larkin's use of the word "lying" immediately begins to undermine this intimate picture. Yes, we imagine two people stretched out side by side. But we also hear another meaning of the verb "to lie": to deceive, to say words that are untrue. The word "lying" introduces the central paradox of the poem; two conditions may exist simultaneously — closeness and the distance of falsity. Moreover, it's important to note that the man and woman aren't simply "lying" but "lying together," the deception mutual and reciprocal.

But Larkin doesn't give the reader too much time to dwell on the multiple meanings of "lying" before he hurries on in the next line to explore the image of a couple in bed. These figures are an "emblem," he explains, a representation "of two people being honest" (3). In other words, this couple lying in bed immediately becomes something larger. The two people are abstraction made flesh. They are allegory. Even as their bodies remain separate and distinct, the bed functions as a frame, visually uniting them. They should be the very picture of connectedness.

This is Larkin, which means that the second stanza opens with the word "yet," another indication that this intimacy is a deception. "Yet more and more time passes silently" (4). We are meant to understand that the man and woman have been in bed for a long while, saying nothing yet wanting to speak. Haven't we all experienced this stretched-out silence? Perhaps, the couple has lain there so many minutes or hours that the outside noises of midnight begin to intrude on the small room. Even the wind blowing against the pane sounds "incomplete" (5), echoing the disquiet of the pair. And, as they remain listening, their ears — or maybe, their imaginations — sharpen. The man and woman begin to picture clouds bunched and split apart by the wind's "incomplete unrest," a union and division that mirrors their own attempts at convergence.

This is high Romanticism, in which the natural landscape reflects the interior lives of unhappy lovers.

As the sentence continues into the third stanza, the couple imagines greater distances: "dark towns heap up on the horizon" (7). These "dark towns" may be populated with dozens of equally unhappy romances. Or, the towns are troubles concretized, with their sharp roofs and blacked-out windows. And then, suddenly, Larkin shifts from a Romantic perspective to that of a Naturalist. "None of this cares for us," he declares flatly (8). For the first time in the poem, the speaker makes it clear that the narrative is personal, not detached third person but first person plural. Us. The speaker is not an unbiased observer but a player involved in the scene he has so meticulously described; he is one of the two actors unspeaking and awake.

"None of this cares for us." Towns are merely towns; if they are dark, it is only because the night lacks a moon or the streetlights have gone out. The dark towns, the wind, all of it remains as unconcerned with human emotion as does the "expensive delicate ship" in W.H. Auden's "Musée des Beaux Arts," which sails "calmly on" despite the fact that a boy named Icarus has just fallen "out of the sky" in a mess of melted wax and snapped wings.

The world beyond the bedroom is neither interested in the suffering of lovers, nor is it able to offer an answer to such suffering. The third stanza ends on enjambment, a sentence building with uncertainty and desolation as it spills into the last tercet of the poem:

> None of this cares for us. Nothing shows why
> At this unique distance from isolation
>
> It becomes still more difficult to find
> Words at once true and kind,
> Or not untrue and not unkind. (8-12)

In bed, the couple should lie at a distance "from isolation," or so the poem claims (9). Isolation stays outside: the clouds, the dark towns, the sharp division of the horizon. The bed should function as a boundary, protecting the lovers. But Larkin's employment of the adjective "unique" when paired with the noun "distance" is striking. The poet does not intend "unique" to mean "rare" or "irreplaceable," as in a unique opportunity or a unique painting. Instead, he is defining the word as the *OED* does: "one and no other; single, sole, solitary." The ninth line becomes in some ways the remotest of the poem, containing as it does, three words — "unique," "distance," and "isolation" — which are variations on the same theme: The loneliness of the individual.

And the final stanza does little to resolve the isolation. Because the bed has transformed into a locus of distance, it is the place where words are now "still more difficult to find" (10). The verb "find" suggests physicality or solidity, language something to be discovered and touched. Words are elusive as the perfect spot on the mattress during a night of insomnia. They are the plumped pillow that keeps flattening out, the cotton sheet continually tangling around an ankle. As if to enact his point, Larkin then elucidates the kind of words difficult to locate, attempting not once but twice to identify them: "Words at once true and kind, / Or not untrue and not unkind" (11-12).

Larkin's use of negation is what makes the final lines of the poem so difficult to pin down: none, nothing, not untrue, not unkind. English teachers often caution students against the double negative. Double negatives are deemed inefficient; they are convoluted, likely to trip the reader as he walks through the sentence. Larkin's "not untrue and not unkind" is an example of litotes, a "figure of speech, in which an affirmative is expressed by the negative of the contrary" (*OED*). With litotes, negation becomes understatement, which in turn becomes irony. Litotes damn with faint praise, as when the French say *c'est pas mal*. The lovers in bed can't find anything to express to one another. They speak neither cruelties nor pallid phrases that barely avoid sounding cruel. "[N]ot untrue and not unkind" means the same as "true and kind." At the same time, Larkin's repetitions of "not" and "un" leave behind the dark connotations of the negative, like a residue deposited on the poem. Despite the litotes' grammatical implications, the reader hears the final phrase as "untrue and unkind." The lovers don't speak, but a whole bedroom full of malice can be inferred.

Because "Talking in Bed" addresses the speech act (or the act of *not* speaking), it's worth noting musical structure. The poem consists of four tercets rhyming *aba cac dcd eee*, which is a kind of backwards terza rima. Rather than following the traditional rhyme scheme of terza rima — *aba bcb cdc etc.* — in which the introduction of each new rhyme poses an opportunity for the poet to expand the established music of the verse, Larkin's interconnected rhymes seem to diminish as they travel down the page: the pairing of "easiest" with "honest" reduced to the unhappy "unrest," or the pairing of "silently" and "sky" narrowing to the uneasy "why" in the next stanza.

And while the interlocking sounds should imply connection and closeness, Larkin's play on *terza rima* also calls attention to the separateness of the paired lines. For instance, the first and third lines of the poem can be read as one complete statement: "Talking in bed ought to be easiest . . . An emblem of two people being honest." And we can link the fourth and sixth lines in a similar manner: "Yet more and more time passes silently . . . Builds and disperses clouds about the sky." Or even the seventh and the ninth: "And dark towns heap up on the horizon . . . At this unique distance from isolation." But, in each stanza, the middle line acts as an intrusion, separating the first and third, preventing them from becoming one thought. A line like "An emblem of two people being honest" remains parallel with "Talking in bed ought to be easiest," simultaneously attached to its antecedent yet unable to touch. Even the closing tercet, with its monorhyme of "find," "kind," "unkind," offers little resolution. The heavy masculine rhyme ought to evoke certainty, but succeeds only in reinforcing the irony of the scene: simple, direct words should be easy to utter. They aren't.

Reading "Talking in Bed," it's difficult not to think of a word like "fidelity," which is as often applied to our manipulation of language as it is to our treatment of a beloved. We are faithful or unfaithful to the truth. We are faithful or unfaithful to one another. What is it these two people don't say in bed? What confessions don't they make? Perhaps fidelity is also the purview of the poet, who must render the details of his narrative so carefully, so faithfully that the poem becomes almost indistinguishable from lived experience.

As I write the first draft of this essay, my husband lies in the bed beside me. The blanket has fallen from him, and I can see the sharp edge of his shoulder blade. We call it his *wing* — that hard angle of bone — because a bicycle accident two years ago left one side a little higher than the other. Sometimes I like to imagine that a second hurt could balance his body out, give him a perfect pair of wings instead of just this one, lopsided effort at flight. He isn't asleep right now but will be soon. Even when we have argued (or, as is the case here, even when we haven't), he can drift from anger into sleep, while I stare at the ceiling all night. I listen to the click of hotel keys in neighboring doors, the laughter of guests in the rooms on either side of us. How close and not unclose all of it seems.

Gilbert Allen

# _My Guardian Biped_

_Absolutely no talking cats!_
— submission guideline

Yes He can, yes He can,
He can open that can.
Open He can

most anything, even
His notsnout, even
this carpeted heaven

He stalks — like He's ready
to sprint up a tree
with pure _joie de vivre_.

But High Muckamuck
moves in slow motion — stuck
on two legs. The poor shmuck.

And His tongue couldn't tweeze
this Lilac Burmese
to pluck out the fleas.

Though it never unwraps
to sandpaper His lips,
it endlessly flaps.

Now He folds, in midair,
to conform to His Chair.
That stare. That stare.

He wants me, right there,
for a lap dance. Oh dear.
That hide with no fur

on One that can't purr.

GILBERT ALLEN

## *"Officials Are Optimistic He Has Been Killed"*

> *— Radio news report, after a surgical strike*
> *in northwestern Pakistan*

Driving, I barely hear — because
on Route 291,
beside the Greenville cemetery,
this afternoon's big wind

has filled the world before my eyes
with real plastic roses.
A winter garden? Lost parade?
Whatever one supposes,

I guess — gas on tires, tires
over the rainbow roil
of slick colors, on striped asphalt.
Oil on oil on oil

on oil. It used to be
alive. This potpourri.

## Gilbert Allen

# *Daughter*

I carried you downstairs, into the car,
and drove your mother to the hospital —
your would-be mother, holding you inside her —
who would've died if you'd have lived a little

longer. We'd have named you for our mothers,
Cecilia and Marie, now vanished too.
What's in a name? Nothing, like a rose
whose scent of absence fills the coming snow.

What I remember: From the seventh floor
I stared at that white desert — till two drivers
oblivious to me and to each other
ominously approaching in reverse

crashed mid-aisle. Got out. What could they say?
They shook their heads, their hands. Drove on their way.

GILBERT ALLEN

# *From an Athlete Dying Young*

We all are. Well, except perhaps
for those extraordinary chaps
whose hearts implode at ninety-one
beholding their first hole-in-one.

As for the rest of us, we die
in rehab or in surgery:
our bodies broken, our mind bent
on misconstruing what they meant.

"The best thing is to play and win,"
said Bobby Riggs to Billie Jean.
His 55-year-old Good News?
"The next best thing's to play and lose."

Track or diamond, field or court,
our time there is, alas, too short.
*Raise?* We can't even don the cup.
And then, at last, we just give up.

But dying once opens the eyes
to earth's impending, dark surprise:
that Lord of Flies, that Final Buzzer
after which there is no other.

Erica Dawson

## *Oklahoma*

I had half a mind for Richie Halverson
(And half for Tony Sims) when Grandpa shot
Himself. He did it in the golden haze,
Bright golden haze, right near a redbud bough,
Right when those two young boys swift-kicked my shins
Under the monkey bars. I swear the bone
Reverberated like aluminum
While rain rusted the roof's crosshatches. Two
Birds and a single stone, it's six and half
A dozen. I should have to know no more.

If only he had done it in November,
Beneath a redbud and bright golden haze,
When, like all romances, we'd all moved on
And that year's leaves were gone with nothing but
A carrion of branches strewn by hungry crows
Looking the least bit murderous. There would
Be nothing for the gun salute to hit
During the funeral, no life to bounce
Against, refrain, and no more boomerang
Of bullets spreading out its reverie.

The *click clack blaow* sounds like what dead sounds like
To children:  tireless, meandering,
Unending like the sidewalk walk to school,
Littered with dormant zoysiagrass and white,
Thick boxes: hopscotch drawn with sloppy chalk,
Where a trove of worms gathers around a slug
Dying in table salt, like its twenty-some
Babies.

If only it were February
When the ground beneath the snow's immunity
Has not one noise to mute.  A winter sky
Could have had enough dark clouds to nigrify
My grandpa's morning black, or blue, to block
The sun, preserve the kind of haze where you
Don't know what day ends where or which one starts.
He could have slept while I outran the boys
And morning lingered in close longitudes.

If only we all lived in Oklahoma.

Who's dew to say that morning needed tears?
Time knows no hurt.
                And who are we to say
The corn is not as high as an elephant's eye,
That all the stars aren't big and bright here, too?

# Erica Dawson

## *Back Matter*

*This jigaboo moves here in shades of green.*

I.

This version, 2.0,
Zion's bad seed, absurdity's
Daughter — I'm talking gangsta. Please.
I'm full of ghetto woe.

All you mamas cry. Please, call
Me too American, too black.
I'm gospel-singing with my back
Up to your front. I'm all

Go with my Nikes on.
*Back: as in "go," sound on the tongue*
*Articulate, well-spoken, hung*
*In the aft of the mouth. Back: gone;*

*Arrears; to bet on. Back:*
*Pertaining to support; to cause*
*Backward movement; chillin', its hems, haws;*
*Brute force strength with no lack-*

*Luster effort.*

II.
       I do
It with my back into it, sweat
My skin, drug formicating, wet —
My fingers scratch it blue.

Hallucinations needle
The skin protecting them. I head
For the EMERGENCY — hot bed,
A microcosmic beetle

Of Cincinnati streets.
Pigs, no doubt, have a man spread-eagle,
Cuffed to a gurney, all the legal
Miranda wrapped in beats

Of EKGS, and blood,
(The point blank gunshot to the chest)
STAT angiectomy, last quest,
Red Jello gummed like cud.


III.


*Back: animal; past due;*
*Belonging to a time* like back
In the day — progress and growth both whack.
*Back; backhand; and, a coup;*

*Defensive player who,*
*Behind the other players, scores*
*First contact. Back:* as in watch yours.
*Back: the body, new —*

*New emperor's clothes. Back: how*
*You know where you have been: Chi; Tao;*
*"Whaddup"* and not *"goodbye"* or *"ciao,"*
But *"Peace"* and *"One." Back: now.*

IV.

Was I the once-green jigaboo
Who, now, sees red? Who, now, sees blue?
Is there a sadness close to true?
What hue is misery?

Can you see me now? I butt
In beats and flows and every nome
And phoneme while I'm going home
To lay back in the cut.

Erica Dawson

# *Intermission*

      *O Mary, don't you weep.*
I got a primo seat up in
The mezzanine. Your song is sin
      It sounds so good, those sweep-

      ing hand snaps, constant beat,
The note that's in between the lung
And top of the mouth, right on the tongue.
      The bass doo-wops compete

      With *Martha, don't you mourn.*
The tan, humongous organ pipes
Tail up the walls. Their flathead stripes
      Make ceiling screws look torn

      As the Red Sea. Forgotten,
Mary? No. Your long note's the crown
Around the blighted army, drown-
      ded, a-singing *Mary*…. cotton-

      White conchs. You hold that note.
A million bones in water skin
Drift with your wakes. Seahorses spin.
      The stage begins to float

      Not to a climax hung
In sound still-life as dead as nature
But life in silent nomenclature.
      The treble S is slung

From the conductor's wrists.
There, in the faltering high C,
The alto's note, sad symmetry
And syllable, subsists

Like absent seagulls who,
Ashore, leave tiny fleeting prints,
As markers of their sustenance,
And hover in the blue.

## Erica Dawson

# *Little Black Boy Heads*

Up at the top there lies a cowlick I
Just got to wrap my finger in, but can't;
Their cuck-a-bucks clipped down to the root; can't pry
One strand loose with a pick. Though I could plant
A kiss, perfect, on their round scalps' short threads
Like splinters on my lips, I'd rather fill
A field with a thousand little black boy heads,
Ascend a white oak high and stare until
Their shorn cowlicks appear to swirl. No hair
Would move, then one by one, the heads would tease
With growing spirals, hypnotize like air-
Embodied branches braced for lift-off. Please,
You stubborn noggins, take your hats off.
                                                    Some
Day when I have my own, I'll palm his skull
And he will nap against my nipple. Thumb
In his soft spots, I'll sing of how I cull
Him from the black field bound beneath a sky
Bright blue, and sun so yellow the whole span
Splays green. His always-girl, I'll sing him, *Fly,*
*Boy, fly. Then run away fast as you can.*

AMY GLYNN

## *Pomegranate*

*Punica granatum*

*For Benjamin Faircloth*

Remember: it was always going to be
like this between us. You were always leaving
and I was always left. The self-deceiving
perception at the heart of tragedy

is simply that it could have been evaded
if we'd known more, if we'd chosen differently.
But this is myth, and the reality
is that it's all decided. Consecrated

before we're born to deities who deal
in rages, jealous whims, lies — we each follow
a script that's peopled with a cast of hollow
supporting players, placed to make you feel

you're choosing things. You never chose. We never
choose. And every story proves it. Look:
one never gets too far in any book
of ancient lore before some far-too-clever

symbolism crowns one with a flower
or fruit that spells out all one's metaphors.
The geode of the pomegranate's yours,
that hand-grenade of tiny, taut-skinned, sour

cabochon garnets. See, it all makes sense:
waxing when you were born and ripe to splitting
the day you died, endlessly retrofitting
the framework that supports all the events

of those two decades. First of all, Demeter
and Persephone — for did you not spend seasons
in some personal hell? And were there ever reasons
for it? Could you have given any neater

explanation, than that you had swallowed
the fruit of the dead? And, not just death, but death-
like sleep, narcosis, shallow breath
smoked with poppy resin. In the hollowed

hexagon of the pomegranate shell
some sculptors saw the lethal opiate
that made the grieving and the sick forget
themselves. It's, tellingly, too tough to tell

at times, whether one symbolized the other
(two seedy capsules overripe with meaning),
or whether visual likeness has us gleaning
mixed messages, and misassuming either

where the other was meant. Death and fertility
are never far apart, and always, fruit
means progeny, means sex. This attribute
the pomegranate wears especially

well: Hera crowned in its calyx on the wall
of an ancient Argive temple, or the speeding
temporal pulse of lovers in a wedding reading
from the Song of Solomon — behind the veil

a stunning ripeness, a fecundity the wind
blows into view. Though, blown, Lorca had found,
still, in the burst fruit's scarlet pulp and rind
the gory blossom of a gunshot wound.

Stilled, you will still recede forever. Gone
from earth at twenty, still you seem somehow
much older, much younger. Still, no matter now.
You made yourself eternal; now I go on

without you. Leather, liquid ruby, pith
like bone shards, strewn in an almost careless way,
except that there is no carelessness in myth.
You were always leaving. It doesn't matter why.

## Amy Glynn

# *Dandelion*

*Taraxacum officinalis*

*"One thing is certain and the rest is lies;*
*The Flower that once is blown for ever dies."*
  — Edward Fitzgerald,
      *The Rubaiyyat of Omar Khyyam*

I'll tell you, friend: time flies. And all
the heavy things grow very light
and fade, like light, part particle,
part wave, all fractional, to white.

Expanding out of density,
trading its vividness for breadth,
something as singular as what
you wish for most, with one good breath

unlatches from you, separates,
multi-directional, a mass
accumulating in reverse,
dispersed. Such structures, feathered, flexed

to seek what suits them, fugitive
in the pursuit of permanence,
are light because they're bloodless. Flight
requires us to be more air

than body. Even voices weigh
too much to carry. That is why
they fade. And so we will — and yet
will not entirely — forget.

What's flown from us is somewhere, still
intent on germinating. Let
it go. The wind can bear it. See
an hour in Eternity

and lighten up. It's later than
you think, babe. Tempus fugit. *You
know how to whistle, don't you, Steve?
Just put your lips together, and*

*Blow.*

Amy Glynn

# *Chamise*

*Adenostoma fasiculatum*

There is no wind. The chaparral has gone
to decadence. And the sun, at such a height,
leaves the sky desiccated, bleached ash-white.
A concentrated brightness, an indrawn

gathering of the light, as if the whole
world were enclosed within a camera
obscura, an inverted replica
universe cynosured through a pinhole.

Even the soil is aching from the heat;
a cracking bed of serpentine where few
species contrive to grow, and those that do
sustain themselves on nothing but complete

famine and drought. More than sustain: they flout
the whole system, responding to the mean
conditions with a kind of libertine
excess, oiling themselves elaborately, without

a care for consequence. Inviting fire.
Anointing their dry leaves with aromatic
resins just to inspire a dramatic
response. Spontaneous combustion. Dire

repercussions, but they've thought of that
too, developing at once two kinds of seed:
one sprouts in wet soil. One is only freed
if the achene is scorched. This habitat

requires certain adaptations. And
rather than being meager in return
for meagerness, why not agree to burn?
Say there is nothing you cannot withstand.

AMY GLYNN

## *Blackberry*

*Rubus fruticosus*

> *"Longing, we say, because desire is full of endless distances."*
> — Robert Hass, "Meditation at Lagunitas"

Isn't this how it always is? The great
tangle. The big yes-but. The sheer
ampleness of things and how
there's always a catch.

Here is the world's elaborate fruitfulness
thrown forth at such a dizzy pace it seems
you could be buried alive in it. It's like
time-lapse photography,

or the temporal distortions of a dream. And the way
the arching canes hold up
their idiot abundance side by side
with those recurved, flexed thorns. There's no free lunch,

you know, even on this long dust-moted trail
where deer and tribes of tule elk
might ruminate on how it always is
with acceptance, with grieving, with surprise.

The trail is lined with brambles. There's a vast
thicket, and yes, it speaks for everything
the trail is, all the crazy plenitude
and all the untraversable, unclosable

distances. And the berries burgeon there and this
is what the poets love, the way there is

no good way to distinguish, at first glance,
the bead of juice from where the berry burst

in your grasp, and the bead of blood
welling from the tiny puncture wound.
The air is scented with the leaves of bay
and coyote bush. This trail only ends

because the ocean stops it.

R.S. GWYNN

# *Dogwatch*

*The North Atlantic*
*March, 1944*

The "happy time" is long past, and the great
Convoy steams eastward at nine knots to fill
Bellies of bombers and of boys whose fate
Will be to seek out other boys to kill.
Or be killed. Twenty-six, my father stands
The dogwatch, and he smokes and looks to sea,
Having this evening folded many hands
And held out for the right card patiently,
Raking a future in with bills and chips.
A flash, a muffled crack, and not much more,
And where, a moment since, one of our ships
Has been, more depths of darkness than before,
And, far behind, a home, a son, a wife,
And, waiting with them to be lived, a life.

# R.S. Gwynn

## *God's Secretary*

*For Robert Archambeau*

Her email in-box always overflows.
Her out-box doesn't get much use at all.
She puts on hold the umpteen-billionth call
As music oozes forth to placate those
Who wait, then disconnect. Outside, wind blows,
Scything green leaves. She sees a sparrow fall,
Fluttering to a claw-catch on a wall.
Will He be in today? God only knows.

She's never seen His face — He's so aloof —
And long resigned He'll neither know nor love her,
She can still wish there were some call, some proof
That He requires a greater service of her.
Fingers of rain now drum upon the roof,
Coming from somewhere, somewhere far above her.

R.S. GWYNN

# Casus Belli

*Pope's* Iliad, III, *205–10*

The impotent old men, gumming their mush
High on the wall and safe from any harms
The Greeks might bear, gape but raise no alarms
When she comes forth, only a reverent hush
In which flesh is remembered. Then a rush
Of cries — *No wonder, such celestial charms*
*For nine long years have set the world in arms! —*
Brings to her throat the faintest tinge of blush.

Far below, Alexandros, Prince of Troy,
Trembles, facing his fire-maned Spartan foe,
And thinks to himself then, if he thinks at all
When he looks back and upward at his joy,
How beautiful a thing she is — but so
Remote at such great height, so pale, so small.

R.S. GWYNN

# *Victor Hugo: So Boaz Slept (Booz endormi)*

Boaz lay down in weariness and pain;
He'd spent long hours laboring on his land
And smoothed his blanket with a dusty hand
To sleep among his heaps of garnered grain.

More fields of wheat stood ready to be mowed;
Though wealthy, he was not an unjust man.
Down his mill-race unclouded waters ran,
And in his forge no hellish irons glowed.

His beard shone silver like a brook in spring.
His sheaves were thick but bundled without greed;
And when, at harvest, gleaners came in need,
He said, "Leave some ears for their gathering."

On righteous paths his feet were known to dwell,
And goodness cloaked him like a robe of white;
His grain poured forth for all whose hungry plight
Touched him, like water from a public well.

Honest with workers, loyal to his kin,
He honored thrift no less than charity;
The women watched old Boaz wistfully
And saw more in him than in younger men.

An old man sees his source with clearer sight;
Soon exiting this world of troubled days,
He holds eternity within his gaze.
A young man's eyes flash fire; an old man's, light.

§

So Boaz slept beneath the moon's faint glow.
Among the great stones massed outside his mill,
His reapers lay together, dark and still,
In that mild evening age on age ago.

Judges still ruled the tribes of Abram's blood.
The Hebrews, wandering in their land of birth,
Saw footprints left by giants in the earth
Soft and damp from the still-remembered flood.

§

Like Jacob, or like Judith, Boaz too
Lay fast asleep upon his humble bed;
The gates of heaven, far above his head,
Half opened, and a dream came passing through.

And from his loins a great oak, flourishing,
Stirred Boaz in his dream, and, gazing down,
He saw a race ascending it; a king
Sang at the roots; a god died in its crown.

Then Boaz murmured with a heartfelt sigh:
*How can it pass that I should bear this tree*
*When eighty years and more have fled from me?*
*I have no son, nor wife to get one by.*
*The woman, Lord, with whom I shared this bed*
*Has gone forever, sharing one with Thee;*
*Yet still we two remain together, she*
*Half-living in my thoughts, and I half-dead.*

*Shall I conceive a nation sprung from me,*
*A tree arising from this ancient dust?*

*Only when I was younger could I trust*
*That day could wring from night such victory;*

*For now I tremble like a winter bough;*
*Alone and widowed, I am dry and old,*
*And as night falls I bend against the cold*
*As to the trough the plow-ox dips his brow.*

Thus Boaz mourned. The cedar does not feel
The rose that clings to it; his dream was sweet
Yet painful to him; and it was so real
He did not sense the woman at his feet.

§

So Boaz slept, while Ruth, the Moabite,
Laid herself at his feet with naked breast,
Hoping he would not wholly waken, lest
He find her there, unknown in the pale light.

But Boaz never knew that she was there,
Nor did Ruth know what God required of her.
The breath of night caused asphodels to stir,
And all Galgala teemed with perfumed air.

Darkness deepened — nuptial, august, sublime.
Perhaps an angel watched them, hovering
Above them with a barely beating wing;
Blue shadows brushed their eyes from time to time.

The breath of Boaz softened like the tones
Sung by stream water when it flows across
A gentle bed of pebbles thick with moss
While lilies bloom among the hilltop stones.

So Boaz slept, and Ruth awakened first
To drowsy sheep-bells tinkling in the night;
The false dawn was aglow with kindly light
In that still hour when lions slake their thirst.

The whole world dreamed, from Ur to Jerimadeth;
Stars studded the blue velvet of the air;
The sickle moon hung low; Ruth said her prayer,
Begging the heavens in her softest breath,

Barely moving, with veiled, half-lidded eyes,
To say what god, what summer harvester,
Had come that night to make his peace with her,
Leaving his golden scythe there in the skies.

# LEN KRISAK

## *Pedestrian*

Straight out of "Trouble": Robert Preston's hands.
Head-high, they wobble like The Music Man's
In warning: DANGER! Lurching from the curb,
A marionette whose parts are purest verb,
He steps off Bolger-scarecrow-like toward Oz
(The other side). It gives us drivers pause
To watch a walk so far outside the norm,
Yet *traffic*'s being held up, *not* this form
Negotiating four lanes all alone,
So why hands-up? The street now all his own,
He staggers with a holy-roller's glee,
A spastic, touchdown-signalling referee
Who wig-wags us he'll soon be where he may
Walk on, hands-down, and we can pull away.

Len Krisak

## *Foyer*

What are the houses of the old?
Last vestibules we enter,
Small vastnesses. They smell of mold,
Of camphor, and of must,
And of necessity, their center
Cannot hold.
Moth-eaten are their rooms
Where merely breathing dooms
Us to incorporating dust,
And to the anterooms that take us in.
Penultimately cold,
We wait there to begin.

# Len Krisak

## *Fit for a Runner*

The wall and ground's hypotenuse, he leans
In hard, with palms against the stone, this boy,
As if he'd push it over: an Achilles
Stretch that looks as if its straining means
That block by block, he plans to press on till he's
Overthrown the topless towers of Troy.

Len Krisak

## *An Italianate Façade*
## *on the Boston Garden*

Around from staggered quoins
Locking the buff-and-butter-colored front and sides,
Down planes of which the dawn sun glides,
And on its public face, where mortar joins

The rusticated brick
To higher stories dressed in almost-ashlar stone,
The posh hotel has held its own.
Light plays on the entablature its trick

Of early-morning cream
Perversely sinking, washing down the curtain wall
To settle, in a silent fall
From penthouse heights, on pavements breathing steam.

Between the window rows,
The free hand of the architect still interposes
A line of bosses cast as roses.
On corbels made to seem like torches pose

Pineapples thrusting through
Split pediments the windows wear — and have so worn
For ages, long before were born
Those passers-by granted the current view.

Timeless as well, the swags
That drape some piers in catenaries, or festoon
The shallow niches now, as noon
Draws near, to lift the shade from sidewalk flags.

But light that melts and seeps
Its way — or tries to — deep inside this rich façade
(And bathes the visage of a god
Who looks perhaps Apollo-like, and keeps

His chin upon a dome
Of canvas standing in for what could be an awning),
And ever since the day's first dawning
Has warmed the masonry in monochrome —

How nearly may it come
To pattern how the spirit moves upon the forms
Of obdurate matter as it warms?
Might not our truest type be taken from

The model of that tower
Set down but barely half a city mile away
And clad in glass for pure display?
It cloaks itself in self-reflecting power,

Sans every ornament
But one, which serves to ward off all that might come near:
Bright, brittle panes where there appear,
Oh, little more than shapes in which are blent

The traffic of a day
And what it's spent. Should these machined and polished squares
That spurn whatever sunlight shares
Then represent, in silicates, our clay?

The meaning-making mind,
So prone to have its say no matter what we will,
May well elect stone's yielding still,
And come to rest on what has been designed

For radiance, surely:
That architrave, pilaster, console, and volute,
Amidst acanthus-tangled fruit,
Have mixed their blessing for us not obscurely,

But plain as each motif
May show. Though clearly not the palace of some Pitti,
It offers to this earthly city
A structure built once out of the belief

That though derivative,
Such forms and shapes embody both some fine ideal
And all the world should take for real,
Seen in the proper light where it must live.

# ACKNOWLEDGMENTS

GILBERT ALLEN. "My Guardian Biped," "'Officials Are Optimistic He Has Been Killed,'" "Daughter," and "From an Athlete Dying Young" are from *Catma*. Copyright 2014. Reprinted with the permission of the author and Measure Press, Inc.
ERICA DAWSON. "Oklahoma," "Back Matter," "Intermission," and "Little Black Boy Heads" are from *The Small Blades Hurt*. Copyright 2014. Reprinted with permission of the author and Measure Press, Inc.
AMY GLYNN. "Pomegranate," "Dandelion," "Chamise," and "Blackberry" are from *A Modern Herbal*. Copyright 2014. Reprinted with permission of the author and Measure Press, Inc.
R.S. GWYNN. "Dogwatch," "God's Secretary," "*Casus Belli*," and "Victor Hugo: So Boaz Slept" are from *Dogwatch*. Copyright 2014. Reprinted with permission of the author and Measure Press, Inc.
LEN KRISAK. "Pedestrian," "Foyer," "Fit for a Runner," and "An Italianate Façade on the Boston Garden" are from *Afterimage*. Copyright 2014. Reprinted with permission of the author and Measure Press, Inc.
PHILIP LARKIN. "Talking in Bed" is from *Collected Poems*. Copyright 2004. Reprinted with permission of Farrar, Straus and Giroux.
RICHARD WILBUR. "Hamlen Brook" is from *Collected Poems 1943-2004* by Richard Wilbur. Copyright © 2004 by Richard Wilbur. Reprinted by permission of Houghton Mifflin Harcourt Publishng Company. All rights reserved.

# Contributors

AUSTIN ALLEN is a poet, essayist, and the Editor-in-Chief of the Poetry Genius project at Rap Genius. His poetry has appeared in *Iron Horse Literary Review*, *The Missouri Review*, *The New Guard*, *Unsplendid*, and elsewhere. His essays have been featured by *Poetry Foundation*, *Open Letters Monthly*, *Big Think*, and other outlets. He lives in New York City.

DICK ALLEN's latest collection, *This Shadowy Place*, was recently released by Saint Augustine's Press and received the 2013 *New Criterion* Poetry Prize. His previous books include *Present Vanishing: Poems* and *The Day Before: New Poems* (Sarabande Books). His work has appeared in *Poetry*, *The New Criterion*, *American Scholar*, and *Cape Rock*, among others.

GILBERT ALLEN's latest collection is *Catma* (Measure Press, 2014). He is also the author of five other collections of poems: *In Everything, Second Chances, Commandments at Eleven, Driving to Distraction*, and *Body Parts*. He is the Bennette E. Geer Professor of Literature at Furman University.

MARK S. BAUER is the author of two chapbooks, *Imperial Days* (Robert L. Barth Publishing, 2002) and *The Gnarled Man Rises* (Scienter Press, 2005). He works as professor of psychiatry at Harvard Medical School and has authored six books, including the anthology, *A Mind Apart: Poems of Melancholy, Madness, & Addiction* (Oxford University Press, 2009).

MARK BLAEUER is a baseball historian and a retired National Park Service ranger. His poems and translations have appeared in *Angle, The Dark Horse, Ezra, Nimrod*, and *The Rotary Dial*, among others. He lives near Hot Springs, Arkansas.

BRUCE BOND is the author of eight books of poetry, most recently *The Visible* (LSU, 2012), *Peal* (Etruscan, 2009), and *Blind Rain* (Finalist, The Poet's Prize, LSU, 2008). His tetralogy of new books entitled *Choir of the Wells* was released from Etruscan Press in 2013. He is a Regents Professor of English at the University of North Texas and Poetry Editor for *American Literary Review*.

JACK BORREBACH lives in Astoria, Queens.

CHRIS BULLARD's manuscript, *Back*, was published in 2013 by WordTech. His poems have appeared in *Rattle, Green Mountains Review, Atlanta Review*, and other journals.

JOSEPH J. CAPISTA has published poems in *Ploughshares, Slate*, and *Smartish Pace*. A two-time Maryland State Arts Council Individual Artist Award Winner, he teaches writing at Towson University.

MARYANN CORBETT's work has appeared in *Southwest Review, 32 Poems, River Styx*, and *The Dark Horse*, among many others. Her first book, *Breath Control*, came out in 2012, and her second, *Credo for the Checkout Line in Winter*, was a finalist for the Able Muse Book Prize.

JAMES COTTON is a graduate student of Italian at the University of Notre Dame. Recently, one of his sonnets won Honorable Mention in *Lyric* magazine's annual awards contest.

ERICA DAWSON's first collection of poems, *Big-Eyed Afraid*, won the 2006 Anthony Hecht Poetry Prize and was published by Waywiser Press in 2007, and her latest is *The Small Blades Hurt* (Measure Press, 2014). Her poems have appeared in *Best American Poetry, Birmingham Poetry Review, Harvard Review, VQR*, and other journals and anthologies. She teaches at the University of Tampa.

JAMES DEMPSEY teaches in the Humanities and Arts Department at Worcester Polytechnic Institute, and his work has appeared in *The Little Apple, The Lyric, Central Mass Magazine*, and *Diner: A Literary Journal*. He is the author of *The Court Poetry of Chaucer: A Facing-page Translation in Modern English*, and *Zakary's Zombies: A Fairy Tale*.

CHRISTINE DESIMONE practices law in San Francisco. Her poems have appeared in *Alaska Quarterly Review, Zyzzyva, Cimarron Review*, and many other journals. Her first full-length collection, *How Long the Night Is*, was published by Lummox.

JEHANNE DUBROW is the author of four poetry collections, including *Red Army Red* and *Stateside* (Northwestern University Press, 2012 and 2010), and is the co-editor of *The Book of Scented Things: 100 Contemporary Poems About Perfume* (Literary House Press, 2014). In 2015, University of New Mexico Press will publish *The Arranged Marriage*. She is the Director of the Rose O'Neill Literary House and teaches creative writing at Washington College.

JENNIFER FANDEL's poetry has appeared in *RHINO*, *The Baltimore Review*, *Calyx*, and *A Face to Meet the Faces: An Anthology of Contemporary Persona Poetry* (University of Akron Press), among others. A freelance writer and editor in St. Louis, she is a poetry reviewer for *ForeWord Reviews* and a contributing editor for *River Styx*.

AMY GLYNN's latest book is *A Modern Herbal* (Measure Press, 2014), and her work has appeared widely in journals and anthologies including *The Best American Poetry*. Among other honors, she has received *Poetry Northwest*'s Carolyn Kizer Award and a Fellowship from the James Merrill House in Stonington, Connecticut.

JACK GRANATH is a librarian in Kansas City.

R.S. GWYNN teaches at Lamar University, where he is University Professor of English and Poet-in-Residence. His work has appeared in many journals, including *The Hudson Review*, *Poetry*, and *The Sewanee Review*. He is the editor of four anthologies of criticism, the *Penguin Pocket Anthology* series, and (with April Lindner) *Contemporary American Poetry*.

JOSEPH HARRISON is the author of two books of poetry, *Someone Else's Name* (2003) and *Identity Theft* (2008). He has received an Academy Award in Literature from the American Academy of Arts and Letters and a Guggenheim fellowship. His next book of poems, *Shakespeare's Horse*, will be published by The Waywiser Press in 2015.

KATIE HARTSOCK's poems have appeared in *Birmingham Poetry Review*, *RHINO*, *Beloit Poetry Journal*, *Southern Indiana Review*, and *Fifth Wednesday*. She lives in Chicago and is a doctoral candidate in Comparative Literary Studies at Northwestern University.

ALESIA THONE HILL is an undergraduate at Lincoln University, Missouri, in Creative Writing and has poems published or forthcoming in *The Columbia College Review* and *The Lindenwood Review*.

CINDY HILL's poems have been published in *Literary Mama*, *PanGaia*, *Sagewoman*, *WildEarth*, *Vermont Life*, and the National Public Radio *Themes and Variations* program.

KATHRYN HINDS' poetry has appeared in *Goblin Fruit*, *14 by 14*, *The Lyric*, and other journals. Her collection *Candle, Thread, and Flute* was published by Luna Station Press. Kathryn teaches composition and early British literature at the University of North Georgia.

GRETCHEN HODGIN's work has appeared in *Rattle, Magma Poetry,* and *Gargoyle.*

JEFF HOLT's work has appeared in *Kin Poetry Journal, Angle, The Raintown Review,* and *Sonnets: 150 Contemporary Sonnets* (Evansville UP, 2005). In 2012, White Violet Press published Jeff's chapbook, *The Harvest.*

STEPHEN KAMPA's work has appeared in *The Yale Review, Cincinnati Review, Subtropics,* and *Poetry Northwest,* among others. His first book, *Cracks in the Invisible,* won the Hollis Summers Poetry Prize and the Florida Book Awards Gold Medal in Poetry. His second book, *Bachelor Pad,* is forthcoming from The Waywiser Press.

LEN KRISAK's books include *Even as We Speak* (Evansville UP, 2000), *If Anything* (WordTech, 2004), *Odes of Horace* (Carcanet, 2006), and *Virgil's Eclogues* (University of Pennsylvania Press, 2010). In 2014, his translation of Ovid's *Amores and Ars Amatoria* will appear from the University of Pennsylvania Press, his *Catullus* from Carcanet Press, and in 2015, his translation of Rilke's *Neue Gedichte* will be published by Boydell & Brewer.

DAVID LANDRUM's poetry has appeared in *Antiphon, Angle, Raintown Review,* and *Shot Glass,* among others.

PHILIP LARKIN was an English poet, novelist, and librarian, and his books of poetry include *The North Ship, The Less Deceived, The Whitsun Weddings,* and *High Windows.* He died in 1985.

SYDNEY LEA, Vermont poet laureate, has recently published *A Hundred Himalayas: Essays on Life and Literature* (U. of Michigan Press, 2012), and his eleventh poetry collection, *I Was Thinking of Beauty* (Four Way Books, 2013).

DAVID LEIGHTTY's poems have appeared in various journals including *Blue Unicorn, The Cumberland Poetry Review, Iambs and Trochees,* and *Light.* Leightty is the founder and publisher of Scienter Press, a small press for poetry.

MARTIN J. LEVINE's poetry has been anthologized in the book *It Is the Poem Singing into Your Eyes,* edited by Arnold Adoff. He lives in Maplewood, New Jersey.

SUSAN MCLEAN is a professor of English at Southwest Minnesota State University. She has published a chapbook of poems, *Holding Patterns*, and a full-length collection, *The Best Disguise*. Her poems and poetry translations have recently appeared in *Light Quarterly*, *Blue Unicorn*, *Mezzo Cammin*, *Per Contra*, and in anthologies such as *Hot Sonnets* and *Villanelles*.

RICHARD MEYER's poems have appeared in various publications, including *Able Muse*, *14 Magazine*, *The Raintown Review*, and *The Evansville Review*. His poem "Fieldstone" was selected as the winner of the 2012 Robert Frost Farm Prize, and his poem "La Gioconda" was awarded top choice in the 2013 Great River Shakespeare Festival sonnet contest.

ANNABELLE MOSELEY is the author of *The Clock of the Long Now* (David Robert Books, 2012), which made The Poetry Foundation's Bestseller List for Contemporary Poetry in July 2012. Her work has appeared in *Able Muse*, *The National Review*, *The Nervous Breakdown*, and *Umbrella*.

RICK MULLIN's collection, *Coelacanth*, was published by Dos Madres Press. His other books include *Soutine* (Dos Madres, 2012) and *Huncke* (Seven Towers, 2010). His chapbook, *Aquinas Flinched*, was published by the Modern Metrics imprint of Exot Books in 2008.

KATHLEEN NAURECKAS' poems have appeared in *Bluestem*, *Light*, and *Willow Review*, among other journals. Finishing Line Press published her chapbook, *For the Duration*, in 2012.

ALAN NORDSTROM is a professor of English at Rollins College. He won the Society of Classical Poets annual poetry contest in 2012.

ROSANNA OH's work has appeared in *The Hopkins Review*, *The Nashville Review*, *The Common*, and other publications. She lives in Madison, Wisconsin.

MICHAEL PEARCE's stories and poems have appeared in *Epoch*, *Shenandoah*, *The Gettysburg Review*, *Ascent*, and elsewhere. He lives in Oakland, California.

JOHN M. RIDLAND's most recent book of poetry is *Happy in an Ordinary Thing* (Truman State UP, 2013), and his poems have appeared in journals such as *The Hudson Review, The Atlantic, The New Yorker,* and *Poetry,* among many others. He teaches in the English Department and the College of Creative Studies at the University of California in Santa Barbara.

ROY SCHEELE is Poet in Residence at Doane College in Crete, Nebraska. "Wilbur's Intricate Simplicity" is his second essay on Wilbur's work to be published in recent years, following the 2008 publication of "'Wyeth's Milk Cans': Richard Wilbur and the Short Poem."

LEE SLONIMSKY has co-authored a chapbook with Katherine Hastings, *Slow Shadow, White Delirium* (Word Temple Press). Individual poems appear in *The Classical Outlook, Mudfish, The Same,* and *Slant.* The latest Lee Carroll novel *The Shape Stealer,* co-authored with Lee's wife Carol Goodman, is out from Tor Books.

SUSAN DE SOLA's poems have appeared in *The Hopkins Review, American Arts Quarterly,* and *River Styx,* among other venues. She is a David Reid Poetry Translation Prize winner and has published a photography/poetry chapbook, *Little Blue Man,* in collaboration with Clive Watkins.

MICHAEL SPENCE has driven public-transit buses in the Seattle area for twenty-nine years. His poems have appeared in *The Hopkins Review, The Hudson Review, The Sewanee Review,* and *Tar River Poetry,* among others. His latest book is *Crush Depth* (Truman State University Press, 2009).

DAVID STEPHENSON's poems have appeared in *Slant, Umbrella,* and *The Lyric.* His book, *Rhythm and Blues,* was published by the University of Evansville Press in 2008.

PETER SWANSON's work has appeared in *The Atlantic, Asimov's Science Fiction, Notre Dame Review,* and *Slant,* among others. He is currently completing a sonnet sequence on all 53 of Alfred Hitchcock's films, and his debut novel, *The Girl With a Clock for a Heart,* is forthcoming from William Morrow.

LEWIS TURCO is a contributor to *Garnet Poems: An Anthology of Connecticut Poetry Since 1776,* edited by Dennis Barone (Wesleyan) and *Take Heart: Poems from Maine,* edited by Wesley McNair (Down

East). His most recent book is *The Book of Forms: A Handbook of Poetics, Including Odd and Invented Forms, Revised and Expanded Fourth Edition* (UPNE).

BOB WATTS is an Assistant Professor in English/Creative Writing at Lehigh University. His first collection, *Past Providence* (David Robert Books, 2005), won the 2004 Stanzas Prize from David Robert Books, and his poems have been published in *Poetry, The Paris Review,* and *reDivider,* among other journals.

MATTHEW WESTBROOK's poems have appeared in *Poetry, The Hopkins Review, Poetry East,* and *Alaska Quarterly Review,* among other journals. He is a two-time recipient of Individual Artist Awards in poetry from the Maryland State Arts Council.

RICHARD WILBUR's books include *Collected Poems: 1943—2004* (2004); *New and Collected Poems* (1988), for which he won the Pulitzer Prize; *Advice to a Prophet and Other Poems* (1961); *Things of This World* (1956), for which he received the Pulitzer Prize and the National Book Award; *Ceremony and Other Poems* (1950); and *The Beautiful Changes and Other Poems* (1947).

DONALD MACE WILLIAMS' poems have appeared in *Tar River Poetry, American Arts Quarterly, Rattle, Anglican Theological Review,* and other magazines. His *Beowulf*-based cowboy poem *Wolfe* was published as a chapbook by Rattle Editions in 2009.

SHERRAINE PATE WILLIAMS is an MFA candidate at Murray State University's Creative Writing Program in poetry and teaches literacy skills to adults full time for Madisonville Community College.

SHANGRILA WILLY is pursuing an M.A. in Poetry and Fiction at The Johns Hopkins University. She has most recently been published in *Lumina, Sugar House Review, Sou'wester,* and *Rattle,* among others.

JAMES MATTHEW WILSON is the author of *The Violent and the Fallen, Timothy Steele: A Critical Introduction, Four Verse Letters,* and many poems, essays, and reviews. He teaches in the Humanities Department at Villanova University.

# THE 2014 HOWARD NEMEROV SONNET AWARD

$1000 Prize

**Final Judge: R.S. Gwynn**

Deadline: November 15, 2014

1) Sonnets must be original and unpublished. No translations. Writers may enter up to twelve sonnets. Sonnet sequences are acceptable, but each sonnet will be considered individually. Entry fee: $3 per sonnet, checks payable to "Measure Press." Entry fees from outside the U.S. must be paid in cash — U.S. dollars — or by a check drawn on a U.S. bank. Author's name, address, phone number, and e-mail address should be typed on the **back** of each entry.

2) Final Judge for the 2014 competition will be R.S. Gwynn. The winning poem and eleven finalist poems will be published in a 2015 issue of *Measure: A Review of Formal Poetry*.

3) Entries must be sent to the address below and postmarked no later than November 15, 2014. Enclose an SASE if you would like to be notified of the contest results. Entries cannot be returned.

Howard Nemerov Sonnet Award
Department of Creative Writing
University of Evansville
1800 Lincoln Avenue
Evansville, IN 47722

# THE 2014 RICHARD WILBUR AWARD

$1000 Prize & Book Publication

**Final Judge: Dick Davis**

Deadline: December 1, 2014

Named in honor of the distinguished American poet Richard Wilbur, the competition welcomes submissions of unpublished, original poetry collections (public domain or permission-secured translations may comprise up to one-third of the manuscript). This biennial competition (even-numbered years) is open to all American poets — those with or without previous book-length publication — except previous recipients of the Richard Wilbur Award. Winning manuscripts will reflect the thoughtful humanity and careful metrical craftsmanship of Richard Wilbur's poetry.

Manuscripts of between 50-100 typed pages may be submitted unbound, bound, or clipped. Manuscripts should be accompanied by two title pages: one with the title of the collection, the author's name, address, email address, and telephone number; and one with only the title. Submitted manuscripts will not be returned.

The entry fee is $25 per manuscript made payable to "The Richard Wilbur Award." The winning manuscript will be published by the University of Evansville Press in 2015. The postmark deadline for submission is December 1, 2014, and manuscripts should be sent to:

The Richard Wilbur Award
Department of Creative Writing
University of Evansville
1800 Lincoln Avenue
Evansville, IN 47722

# THE TENTH ANNUAL
# ANTHONY HECHT POETRY PRIZE

A prize of $3,000 and publication by The Waywiser Press in the USA and the UK is given annually for a first or second poetry collection. The winner will give a reading at the Folger Shakespeare Library in Washington D.C. in the Fall of 2015, where he or she will appear with the tenth contest's judge.*

Submit a manuscript of between 48 and 88 pages with a $25 entry fee ($27 for online submissions) by December 1, 2014.

Visit the press's website for guidelines and entry forms:

http://waywiser-press.com/hechtprize10.html

or else send an SASE to:

The Waywiser Press
[Anthony Hecht Poetry Prize]
P.O. Box 6205
Baltimore MD 21206

* The contest's previous judges were: J. D. McClatchy, Mary Jo Salter, Richard Wilbur, Alan Shapiro, Rosanna Warren, James Fenton, Mark Strand, Charles Simic and Heather McHugh.

CPSIA information can be obtained
at www.ICGtesting.com
Printed in the USA
FFOW05n1303080914